# Big Questions for Young Minds

## Extending Children's Thinking

**Janis Strasser and Lisa Mufson Bresson**

National Association for the Education of Young Children
Washington, DC

# naeyc®

National Association for the Education of Young Children
1313 L Street NW, Suite 500
Washington, DC 20005-4101
202-232-8777 • 800-424-2460
NAEYC.org

## NAEYC Books

Senior Director, Content Strategy and Development
*Susan Friedman*

Editor-in-Chief
*Kathy Charner*

Senior Creative Design Manager
*Audra Meckstroth*

Senior Editor
*Holly Bohart*

Publishing Manager
*Francine Markowitz*

Creative Design Specialist
*Malini Dominey*

Associate Editor
*Rossella Procopio*

Through its publications program, the National Association for the Education of Young Children (NAEYC) provides a forum for discussion of major issues and ideas in the early childhood field, with the hope of provoking thought and promoting professional growth. The views expressed or implied in this book are not necessarily those of the Association.

Chapters without specified authors are by Janis Strasser and Lisa Mufson Bresson. The following chapters are adapted from articles by Lisa Mufson Bresson and Janis Strasser previously published in the specified issues of *Teaching Young Children*: Chapter 14, "Using Bloom's Taxonomy—Kick-Starting the School Year! Preschoolers Exploring Change Through Long-Term Studies" (August/September 2016); Chapter 15, "How New Materials and the Right Questions Can Extend Preschoolers' Thinking" (December 2015/January 2016); Chapter 16, "'Not All Done, Just Done for Today!' Using Multiday Creative Explorations and Bloom's Taxonomy to Extend Preschoolers' Thinking" (February/March 2016); and Chapter 18, "Bloom's All Around the Room: Using Classroom Displays as 'The Third Teacher' to Inspire Higher-Level Reflective Questioning" (April/May 2016). Sections of the Introduction and Chapter 1 are adapted from "Moving Beyond *Who, What, When, Where,* and *Why*" (October/November 2015).

## Photo credits

Copyright © iStock: cover, vi, 5, 12, 18, 24, 27, 42, 45, 50, 53, 56, 59, 62, 65, 68, 71, 74, 77, 80, 82, 86, 119, 122, 125, 128, 136, 144, and 149

Copyright © Lisa Mufson Bresson: 106, 108, and 111

Copyright © Bob Ebbesen: 7 and 39

Copyright © Megan King: 30, 33, 95, and 98

Copyright © Vera Wiest: 3, 15, 21, 36, 92, 112, 114, 117, and 131

Courtesy of Lisa Mufson Bresson and Janis Strasser: 100 and 103

Courtesy of Kristie Redner: 89

Library of Congress Control Number: 2017947056

ISBN: 978-1-938113-30-7

Item 1132

# Contents

As you ask children questions, remember to really listen to their responses. As an active listener, demonstrate your interest in the children's ideas and your openness to different possibilities rather than listening for the expected, "right" answer.

—Rebecca Isbell and Sonia Akiko Yoshizawa, *Nurturing Creativity: An Essential Mindset for Young Children's Learning*

# Introduction

This book is about high-level questions and how they inspire higher-level thinking in young children. As a preschool teacher and teacher trainer, Lisa has discovered how exciting it is when teachers engage children in high-level thinking. Janis, in her work with teachers, sees how they often struggle to develop and use questions that go beyond eliciting rote answers. We wanted to provide some guidance to teachers because we both saw how their comfort with and knowledge of using higher-level questions impacted the quality of their teaching and learning.

We first began writing about high-level questions in a series of articles for *Teaching Young Children*. We learned that many people were using our articles for staff development trainings. After the publication of the fourth article in the series, which focused on using classroom displays to inspire higher-level, reflective questions (see Chapter 18), a Head Start teacher shared with us the impact that article had on her, saying, "It was like a big door opened in front of my eyes or a huge light shined in the darkness of my mind. I could not believe how important and helpful those questions could be."

That is the purpose of this book. With some practice, when teachers use high-level questions, they too can open doors for children to think about and express more complex ideas.

## Bloom's Taxonomy and the Model for This Book

In 1956, Benjamin Bloom and his collaborators created what is now called Bloom's Taxonomy. A *taxonomy* is a system of classification. Bloom wanted to provide educators a way to classify thinking, understanding, and learning and to measure and organize what they teach. This taxonomy consisted of six levels of cognition, ordered from the simplest to the most complex (Bloom 1956; Fusco 2012):

**Knowledge**—recalling facts or other information

**Comprehension**—simple understanding

**Application**—inferring, or applying information from one situation to another

**Analysis**—breaking down parts from the whole and understanding their relationships

**Synthesis**—putting together parts to make meaning

**Evaluation**—making judgments about the value of something

Over the years, many educational theorists have reinterpreted Bloom's Taxonomy. Almost 50 years after Bloom first created the taxonomy, Lorin Anderson and David Krathwohl (2000) incorporated a fresh perspective. They considered the advances in education over the years as well as the evolution of teachers' thinking about teaching, learning, and assessing their students. They kept somewhat similar categories but substituted *evaluation*, the final level, with *create*. This modified version of the taxonomy, which we will continue to refer to as Bloom's Taxonomy, is the model used in this book because we believe that creating is the critical component that brings the taxonomy to life. The table below compares the two versions.

### A Comparison of the Two Versions of the Taxonomies

| Bloom's Taxonomy (original) | Bloom's Taxonomy (with Anderson & Krathwohl modifications) |
| --- | --- |
| Knowledge | Remember |
| Comprehension | Understand |
| Application | Apply |
| Analysis | Analyze |
| Synthesis | Evaluate |
| Evaluation | Create |

Teachers often use Bloom's Taxonomy to ask children a range of questions, including those that prompt children to recall and understand what they've learned, apply the information, and do something new with it. Although children do not necessarily move in a systematized way through the levels of cognition (from lowest to highest in order), the taxonomy illustrates that children need a foundation in basic facts and information to be able to use their knowledge at a higher level. The higher levels of the taxonomy help *teachers* understand how to ask children thoughtful questions that scaffold and extend their learning, encouraging them to think more critically.

While it's vital to encourage children to think at a higher level, all levels of questions have value. Remembering information is the foundation children need to be able to answer higher-level questions, such as "How will you figure out how many plates we need on the table for lunch?" And children need to *remember* that there are three little pigs and a big, bad wolf and *understand* that the pigs have to figure out how to build strong houses before they can *create* new characters and a new ending. As you get to know each of the children you work with, you can use these categories as a guide to help you scaffold their thinking

and learning. This is particularly important to consider when you work with a child who does not yet have much expressive language or experience answering more complex questions or with children who are dual language learners.

## Using This Book

This book is a practical resource for all early childhood professionals who work with children ages 3 through 6 years in classrooms or family child care settings, higher education faculty who work with preservice or graduate-level early childhood teachers, principals or directors of early childhood programs to use with their staff, and families who want to support their children's learning. The chapters focus on how to integrate high-level questions into the many ways adults interact with young children: in the interest areas of the classroom or family child care setting, during different parts of the daily routine, and while engaging in other learning opportunities. The ideas build on Bloom's Taxonomy, our combined extensive experience with young children, and the expertise of our esteemed colleagues who served as contributing authors.

Each chapter provides specific tips for getting started and three examples of questions at each of the six levels of questioning (Remember, Understand, Apply, Analyze, Evaluate, Create). These sample questions will help you think about the types of questions, statements, or comments that are most likely to elicit the thinking you want children to engage in. Each chapter also includes a list of children's books that support the use of high-level questions ("The Picture Book Connection"). Throughout the book, we have included many clear, useful tips and strategies.

## Part 1: Using Questions in Classroom Interest Areas

Chapters 1–6 describe how to use high-level questions in the basic interest areas of preschool and kindergarten classrooms.

## Part 2: Using Questions During Other Parts of the Daily Routine

Chapters 7–12 discuss the use of high-level questions during other parts of the daily routine: class meetings, read-alouds, music time, large motor activities, outdoor time, and mealtimes.

## Part 3: More Learning Opportunities with Questions

Chapters 13–19 offer ideas for how to use high-level questions on a daily basis in a variety of contexts (such as supporting emotional development during the first months of school, helping children understand diversity, and introducing new materials) and perhaps some new ways to support high-level thinking you hadn't thought about before (during multiday explorations, starting off the school year with long-term studies, with classroom displays, and documenting children's learning).

## Part 4: Resources

The resource section contains examples of how to talk to children using questions at all levels in a wide range of situations. There are also questions that can be cut out, laminated onto index cards, put on a ring, and placed around your classroom, in your pocket, or wherever you can easily refer to them. We have also included some reflection questions about the chapters and themes of the book and a list of print and online resources. For families, there are reproducible handouts that encourage the use of high-level questions when talking to their children about their day, during mealtimes, and while reading bedtime stories.

## What Are High-Level Questions and How Do They Support Young Children's Thinking?

Think about these two questions:

> *What three things do you know about the way young children learn?*
>
> *How would you design a collage that shows the most important things about the way young children learn?*

What kind of thinking does each of these questions require? For the first—which represents the lowest level of question in Bloom's Taxonomy, *remember*—you would probably access a list you already have somewhere in your memory, either from information you learned or from your own experience with children. But the second question (the highest level, *create*) requires you to think in a new way—you likely don't have a ready-made answer and would engage in some higher-level, complex, and creative thinking. Similarly, when you ask young children basic recall questions, such as how many pigs are in the story of *The Three Little Pigs* or what color the wolf is, the answers to those questions don't require much thinking. If a child can't answer those questions, you might learn that she doesn't yet know numbers or colors, or that she wasn't interested in the story. But if you want to engage children in rich cognitive experiences and understand how they think, you might ask, "How would you describe the wolf?" or "How might the three pigs have built different houses if they were fish?" It can be challenging to develop and ask high-level questions ("If you could come to school any way you wanted, how would you get here? Why?") instead of lower-level questions ("How did you get to school this morning?"), but it is well worth the effort!

## What High-Level Questions Aren't—and Are

A high-level question is *never* a yes-or-no question ("Do you have a pet?"). It is never a question that has an obvious answer ("How many wheels does that car have?"). Nor is it a question that has only one answer ("How old are you?"). The answers to those kinds

of questions may demonstrate that children understand language, are paying attention, and can count or identify numbers, colors, or shapes, but the questions don't offer opportunities for children to think very deeply.

Creating a solid base of content knowledge is important—children need to remember information before they can understand it; they must understand it before they can apply it. But you want children's learning to be deeper and more complex. Asking questions that invite them to apply what they've learned or evaluate something encourages them to express their unique ideas. Consider the difference in responses given by a group of kindergartners when shown a mug and asked, "What is this?" Most replied that the object was a cup or a mug. But when asked what they liked about the mug, Julia responded, "It has so many blue swirly rings on it, and I love the big handle." And Juan said, "It's like my abuela's cup. She always puts cinnamon tea and honey in it when I visit her in Puerto Rico."

A high-level question is *always* a question that each child will answer in her own way, which indicates that she is using what she knows and what she's learning instead of just recalling rote information. If it is an effective question, a child will be excited to give you lots of details in her answer and is likely to use complex language. For example, when 3½-year-old Kerry was asked to describe her pet, she said that he was "really, really big and his tongue is always dripping and his tail bangs into the coffee table." And when a group of 4-year-olds was asked to describe the most important things about being 4, they came up with a long list of individual accomplishments and privileges, such as "You can stay up late to watch the moon" and "You can somersault and jump up to the sky."

High-level questions encourage children to expand their thinking and perspective on a subject. Fifteen students in a kindergarten class were asked to discuss this question in pairs: "If you could design a car that could go really fast, what would it look like and why?" The students engaged in long discussions, sketched their answers, and debated which of their car prototypes would be the best and why. Sarah said, "It would have jet-propelled giant engines and go faster than the Flash," and Jared said, "My car has wings and flies higher than a helicopter, and it is sparkly black and red with four hundred and twelve lights."

Most importantly, a high-level question is developmentally appropriate for the age and stage of the individual child. Most 3-year-olds are primarily concrete thinkers. This means that their speech and thinking are quite literal, often focusing on what is physically in front of them. Some 3-year-olds might not be able to answer the more complicated questions that older children can. Children begin thinking more abstractly around age 4 (Copple & Bredekamp 2006).

Teachers can address every stage of development, from the very concrete thinkers to the more developed abstract thinkers, by using Bloom's Taxonomy as a guide to engage in focused lines of questioning. For example, observing a group of 4-year-olds pretending that a stick they found outside is a fork or spoon, you might ask, "What kinds of foods would

be easy or difficult to eat with your new kind of utensil?" If you saw a 3-year-old using the same stick to poke holes or make a line in the dirt, you could say, "Tell me about the marks you are making on the ground." Another approach is to simply make an observation about what you notice in children's play to start a dialogue. For example, to the 4-year-olds you could say, "I see you created a new utensil!" Or, for the 3-year-old, "I see you making such interesting marks in the dirt with that stick."

It's up to you, the one who knows your students best in an educational setting, to decide which questions are appropriate for which children during a particular interaction. Although not all preschoolers and kindergartners will understand some of the higher-level concepts, you can still ask questions that prompt them to think in those ways. For example, instead of "How many carrots are in this bunch?," you might ask Hannah whether she has enough carrots for the teacher, herself, and a nearby child to have one each, and how she knows the answer. If this is too difficult for the child, you might scaffold the learning by helping Hannah count the carrots and the number of people, and then ask whether there are enough for everybody to have one.

Children develop at different rates and may surprise you with their answers. Sometimes, scaffolding these questions by pairing children up or asking questions in small group or whole group settings can be beneficial for those children who aren't ready to answer by themselves. Keep in mind that statements like "I wonder . . ." ("I wonder why that happened") or "Tell me how . . ." ("Tell me how you would change it the next time") also encourage thinking, even though they don't have a question mark at the end!

## Step Up Your Questioning Techniques

The "Step Up Your Questioning Techniques!" graphic on page 9 is based on Anderson and Krathwohl's (2000) work and helps you visualize what using high-level questions with young children looks like based on our model. At each successive level, the questions become more difficult and require deeper thinking from children. Remember that children are not necessarily "at" one step or another in their development—rather, their level of thinking shifts as they are exposed to new experiences and concepts, try out ideas, and make adjustments to what they've already learned. A 4-year-old may be able to experiment and infer on a topic she has a lot of experience with, but when exploring a topic that's new to her, she may spend a lot of time gaining basic facts and understanding and applying what she learns.

Keep these things in mind when you ask children questions:

» **Plan your question, thinking about where your students are developmentally.** Do they have the vocabulary to be able to describe a sunset?

» **Consider their prior knowledge.** Do they know what a dinosaur is? Have they ever been to a pizza place?

» **Try starting a question with "I wonder . . . " or "What do you notice . . . "** These kinds of questions open the door for thinking and observing in depth.

» **Don't be afraid to use big "juicy" words** like *choreograph*, *gizmo*, *vertical*, *segregation*, *document*, *reflect*, *accessory*, *skyscraper*, and *ornithologist*. The children will figure them out in context and their vocabularies will soar!

### Higher-Level Thinking Is Thinking that Makes Your Brain Stronger

Here are some ways you might describe higher-level thinking to preschoolers and kindergartners. Ask them for their own explanations, too!

- "It makes your brain stronger."
- "It's like exercise for your mind."
- "It's like looking at things with a magnifying glass, or (for tech-savvy preschoolers and kindergartners) zooming in on a photo."
- "We are taking our ideas from up here (pointing to head) and bringing them to life with _____ (crayons, blocks, playdough, our bodies)."

### What Is a Good Listener?

Children know when adults are truly interested in what they have to say. When asked their criteria for judging if someone is a good listener, elementary-age children said that the person

- Makes eye contact appropriately
- Is patient and does not interrupt
- Asks questions in a pleasant tone
- Is responsive both verbally and nonverbally
- Prepares for listening by focusing attention on the speaker (Jalongo 2008)

# Step Up Your Questioning Techniques!

**6** **Create**
"What kind of animal can you make that no one else has ever seen before?"

**Children will**
- Make
- Construct
- Design
- Author

**5** **Evaluate**
"What are some reasons why this animal would/wouldn't make a good pet?"

**Children will**
- Express opinion
- Judge
- Defend/criticize

**4** **Analyze**
"How is the animal the same as our pet rabbit?"

**Children will**
- Recognize change
- Experiment
- Infer
- Compare
- Contrast

**3** **Apply**
"Where else have you seen this animal?"

**Children will**
- Explain why
- Dramatize
- Identify with/relate to

**2** **Understand**
"Tell us about the animal."

**Children will**
- Describe
- Discuss
- Explain
- Summarize

**1** **Remember**
"What animal is this?"

**Children will**
- Identify
- Name
- Count
- Repeat
- Recall

» **Make sure to allow plenty of wait time for them to process what you are saying, think about it, and answer.** Give them at least two to three seconds, but vary this according to the needs of the student. (Count "1 Mississippi" for each second.)

» **Ask another question or make a comment** after a child answers. Say, "What else can we add to that?" or "Tell me more about that."

» **Remember to listen** after you ask a question. Use active listening strategies: make eye contact, encourage children to share their ideas, and restate or summarize what they say.

Dual language learners (DLLs), or children who grow up learning two (or more) languages, may not yet have the vocabulary to answer some questions in English. However, researchers have found that "growing up with two languages enhances cognitive flexibility and the ability to use working memory as children go back and forth between their two languages" (Galinsky & Gardner 2017, 7). As you would with any child, start with simple, lower-level questions and gradually ask more difficult questions when you see the child responding easily. If you or another adult speaks the child's home language, ask questions in that language, or invite another child to translate. High-level thinking and speaking will develop in the child's home language before it does in English. See "Working with Children Who Are Dual Language Learners" above for additional tips about supporting DLLs with high-level questions.

### Working with Children Who Are Dual Language Learners

- Support the development of a child's home language and English skills by trying to find an adult, peer, or older child who can speak and ask him questions in his home language.*

- Recognize that sometimes the child may feel shy about responding in English.*

- Use lots of gestures, pictures, labels, and other supports to clarify questions.*

- Allow extra time for the child to process the question.*

- Ask families to help you learn a few questions, such as "What do you think will happen next?" and "How did your strategy work?" in each child's home language. Use a smartphone or tablet to record the child's responses. Save the recording and ask for help translating it to track how the child's responses develop over time.

*Adapted from Nemeth 2012

# Using Questions
# in Classroom
# Interest Areas

The question was not *how* would I enter [the children's play] but, rather, *what* were the effects of my intervention? When did my words lead the children to think and say more about their problems and possibilities, and when did my words circumvent the issue and silence the actors? When did my answers close the subject?

—Vivian Paley, "On Listening to What the Children Say," *Harvard Educational Review*

# Dramatic Play Area

The children in Ms. Liggieri's mixed-age preschool classroom are playing in the interest areas of their choice. In the dramatic play area, 5-year-old Josie dons a red satin kimono embroidered with birds and ties a long piece of blue-sequined fabric around her head. The finishing touch is a striped necktie from the costume basket, which she puts on over the kimono. She then stands in front of a large mixing bowl, stirring intently as she dumps in every piece of pretend food, a collection of smooth river rocks from the science area, several Unifix cubes from the math area, and a handful of pom-poms from the classroom makerspace.

Giuseppe sits at the table next to the bowl with a notepad in front of him, scrawling numbers and letter-like shapes across the page in blue crayon. "You gotta keep mixing!" he excitedly tells Josie.

Ms. Liggieri notices the mixture of toys taken from all over the room in Josie's bowl. Her first instinct is to ask the children not to jumble so many toys from different areas together, but before speaking, she sits by them and quietly observes their play. She notices that each time Josie adds a new toy to the bowl, Giuseppe makes a mark on the notepad. She quickly realizes that the two have created a highly complex play scenario that involves not only role playing and creative costumes but math and literacy as well.

"What are you making, Josie?" asks Ms. Liggieri.

"It's soup!" Josie exclaims. "I'm mixing and Giuseppe is doing the recipe. He's my helper cook, and all our friends are coming over for the party." She motions to the crib where they have lined up all of the dolls, an aspect of the play that Ms. Liggieri hadn't noticed.

Instead of asking a simple question like how many people are coming to the party or what color Josie's kimono is, the teacher decides to follow Josie's lead and asks how Josie got the idea to make a recipe.

Ms. Liggieri then asks if she can help them prepare for their party. Giuseppe tells her to take care of the babies. Ms. Liggieri engages in play with the pair for 15 minutes, mindful not to disrupt or direct their play, and asks them several open-ended questions about the math and literacy aspects they have incorporated into their party preparations. As she moves toward another group of students, she makes a note to go back to the dramatic play area during cleanup time with the containers for the materials Josie has used. She plans to engage the children in a sorting activity using the labels on the containers as they deconstruct the toy soup they have made for the party.

The world of pretend play is limitless. Young children can become so completely immersed in fantasy scenarios that everything around them falls away as they explore the inner world of their imaginations. The dramatic play area provides a wealth of opportunities for engaging in high-level questioning, especially when you ask questions that help children explore complex human dynamics that are a part of their daily lives. Children often act out things they have seen at home, on television, or in their community, and thoughtful questioning can help you understand what their play is reflecting and why it's important to them. If you witness a child in the dramatic play area spanking a baby doll, for example, your instinct might be to say, "That's not nice. Don't do that!" Instead, take a step back and try to understand why the child is acting this out. Most likely, it is because she has seen someone model this behavior, has experienced it herself, or is just acting out her own frustrations—perhaps toward a new baby sibling—in a safe, pretend scenario. Acknowledging the child's feelings with a comment and question such as "I see you are very angry with the baby. What happened to make you feel that way?" opens the door for the child to discuss her emotions. For children, there are no "bad" imaginary play scenarios— only opportunities for both you and them to gain a deeper understanding of their world and the possibilities it presents.

## Getting Started

Before you take the first steps into high-level questioning during pretend play, remember that pretend play *must* be honored as a valuable and legitimate form of expression for children. Just as speaking and writing are forms of communication and expression, pretend play is a language they use to communicate and make sense of the world around them and one of the highest forms of play a child can engage in. When you see children's time in the dramatic play area as a valuable opportunity to better understand children, you can support their high-level thinking and learning.

It is not uncommon to walk into the dramatic play area, sit down, and suddenly feel at a complete loss for what to say. In a situation like this, instead of blurting out "What are you doing?" or "That's such a pretty dress!" often the best solution is to say nothing. Until you feel that you have something to say or ask that will support or expand the children's learning, just listen and observe. Once you think you understand what the play scenario is all about, you can offer brief comments or questions.

When joining in children's pretend play, make sure you do not take over the play; rather, consider how you can extend the learning within the world the children have already created. For example, after you have observed children's play for a few minutes, you could say, "Tell me about what you've created here," or "I wonder why you lined up these chairs like this," to get a better understanding of what their play involves. If you see several children pretending to eat out of bowls with spoons and immediately say, "Oh, are you eating ice cream? Let's make our own ice cream! I'll get some bowls and mixing spoons and all of the ingredients we need," the children's play scenario is no longer their own. You have changed their plans and stopped their exploration into their own imagination by giving them *your* idea about the direction of their play. Instead, ask questions that offer a balance between extending children's existing line of play and inspiring new play, such as "It looks like you're eating something out of that bowl. Can you give me some clues about what's in there so I can try to guess?"

## Supporting Children's Play and Learning

Children's pretend play also reflects their developmental levels. A child who has just turned 3 years old and is just beginning to understand abstract thinking might hold up a wooden spoon to her ear and pretend it is a cellphone, while a child who is about to turn 5 years old might spend a full hour immersed in a complex imaginary scenario filled with role playing, colorful dialogue, and self-made props, similar to Josie and Giuseppe's play in the opening vignette. Some children will move in and out of character to provide instructions to other players. Others will have a harder time integrating their friends into an already-established scenario.

Asking children thoughtful questions or describing something you notice about their imaginary play allows them to think more deeply about the scenario they have created. It also gives them the opportunity to think about the connections they have made as well as make new ones. After observing a child wearing a headscarf as part of a group's pretend play, you might ask, "Where have you seen this type of headscarf before?" to help the children think about the inspiration behind their play. Or, to encourage math learning, you might ask, "I see there are four plates set up at the table, and you said five baby dolls are coming to your party. How will you make sure each baby has a plate?"

## Reigniting Children's Direction and Interest

If activity in the dramatic play area was once robust and high level but seems to have waned, or if you find a child wandering in the area with no real focus, consider the following:

- **Are the materials still interesting?** Consider adding old cameras, cellphones, costume jewelry, or sunglasses to the area. Occasionally rotate some items in and out.

- **Are there enough materials?** There should be enough materials so that three or four children can engage in play with dolls, eat pretend meals, dress up, etc.

- **Is pretend play unfamiliar to this child?** Is she still primarily a concrete thinker? For example, maybe she is not yet able to think about using the collection of bottle caps as part of a soup or making a checkered tablecloth into a fancy party dress.

- **Is the child having difficulty integrating into existing play?** Reflect on the child's prior experiences at home, his language development, and the social dynamics that exist in your classroom.

Providing a place for creative imaginary play is an important function of the dramatic play area. As a reflective practitioner, periodically reassess what materials are available and how children are using them. Then, engage with children in high-level questioning as they explore their roles to understand their world, which helps them build a strong foundation of learning for years to come.

### The Picture Book Connection

*Lion Lessons*, by Jon Agee

*Shhhhh! Everybody's Sleeping,* by Julie Markes

*Stone Soup,* by Marcia Brown

*Tortillas and Lullabies/Tortillas y Cancioncitas,* by Lynn Reiser

*Where the Wild Things Are,* by Maurice Sendak

# Expand Children's Thinking and Learning by Asking Questions

## 1 Remember
(identify, name, count, repeat, recall)

- What color is this vegetable?
- How many dimes are in this cash register?
- What color is that scarf you chose?

## 2 Understand
(describe, discuss, explain, summarize)

- What did you put in the bowl first? next? last?
- Describe the flowers you put in your flower shop.
- Are you and Dino part of the same family? How are you related?

## 3 Apply
(explain why, dramatize, identify with/relate to)

- I see you're setting up all of the different hairstyling products and tools in your hair salon. Show me how you will use some of them on your customers' hair.
- Now that you are the grandmother in the family, how can you get the babies to stop crying?
- When have you seen this kind of menu before?

## 4 Analyze
(recognize change, experiment, infer, compare, contrast)

- How do you think you could turn this piece of fabric that your mom gave us into a piece of clothing for dress-up?
- How can you get the same amount of soup into each of these bowls? How do you think you'll be able to tell if all the bowls have the same amount of soup?
- How can we use this pencil and notebook to help you organize which patients you see first in the animal hospital?

## 5 Evaluate
(express opinion, judge, defend/criticize)

- Which of these tools do you think is the best choice for making your customers' hair curly in your hair salon? Why?
- Which is your favorite scarf in this basket? Why do you like it so much?
- How do you think Mayumi is feeling since you told her she can't be part of the doctor's office you set up here?

## 6 Create
(make, construct, design, author)

- Let's use some classroom materials to design something that helps the baby doll sit higher up at the table so you can feed her more easily.
- Everyone seems to be having a hard time remembering where these materials go at cleanup time. What types of labels can we make that would help everyone know where to put materials away?
- I wrote down the story you were telling your patient when she said she was afraid of the dentist. Maybe you can illustrate the story and we can make a book.

Alternating asking questions with listening attentively will help you determine the appropriate time to ask a thoughtful question.

—Rebecca Isbell and Sonia Akiko Yoshizawa, *Nurturing Creativity: An Essential Mindset for Young Children's Learning*

# Block Area

Rosanne Regan Hansel

2

Five-year-old Luciana wants to use the unit blocks to build a train station like the one that she passes on the way to school every day. Her teacher, Ms. DaNita, listens to Luciana explain her idea and asks her to say more about it.

**Luciana:** I'm trying to make it strong like the brick house in *The Three Little Pigs,* so when the trains rumble in, they won't knock the building down.

**Ms. DaNita:** I noticed that when you first started, your building kept falling down. What will you do this time to make your building stronger, so it doesn't fall down?

**Luciana:** This time I'll put the long blocks on the bottom and then stack the smaller blocks very carefully on top.

**Ms. DaNita:** That sounds like a good plan. Would it help if you look at the photos of the buildings we took when we went on our neighborhood walk to see if you can find a picture of the train station?

**Luciana:** (looking through the binder of photos from the neighborhood walk) Yes, I found it! Look! The train station is kind of square and not as tall as a skyscraper. Oh, and it has cylinder shapes in front of it like these (as she holds up two wooden cylinders).

**Ms. DaNita:** They are called columns. How many cylinder-shaped columns do you see in the photo?

**Luciana:** (pointing to the photo as she counts) Six!

**Ms. DaNita:** Okay! Are you ready to get started?

In the opening vignette, Ms. DaNita models skilled listening as she helps Luciana flesh out her ideas for building a train station. By being fully present during Luciana's play with blocks and responding appreciatively to her efforts by noticing what she is building and asking questions, the teacher shows Luciana that she values her work. Taking this important first step, observing and commenting on children's play, sets the stage for expanding on the ideas children are exploring.

## Getting Started

When you ask open-ended questions, you encourage deeper engagement and thinking to help children remember, understand, apply, analyze, and evaluate as they build and create with blocks. To encourage children to discuss what they're doing in more detail, you can describe what you see or simply say, "Tell me more," as Ms. DaNita did. As important as questions are, however, it takes practice to avoid the pitfall of asking too many questions. Ms. DaNita is careful to focus on Luciana's ideas and give Luciana resources to stretch her thinking. Even the lower-level question the teacher asks—"How many cylinder-shaped columns do you see in the photo?"—is designed to encourage Luciana to seek resources that might help her build her structure more successfully.

## Supporting Children's Play and Learning

Knowing when and how to ask good questions requires preparation. Developing a list of open-ended questions specifically for block building (such as those suggested in this chapter) and posting them where you can easily refer to them is a good starting point. As you become more skillful and comfortable with asking questions, targeted questions will arise more spontaneously as you observe and interact with children. You can have thoughtful conversations with children while they're building in the block area, when they're drawing their block structures, and during group discussions as they revisit or reflect on their work.

### During Building

Keep children safe in the block area by setting up expectations for building behaviors early on and by giving children supports and time to practice the rules. These rules usually include using blocks only for building and deconstructing a child's own construction (Tunks 2009). When children have learned these basic rules for building in the block area and are successfully engaged in creative block play, it is tempting to redirect your attention to other areas of the classroom. Try to resist that temptation! When you take the time to notice what children are building, who they are playing with, what problems they are encountering, what they are discovering about the properties of blocks, and what interests they are expressing, it will help you ask questions that will keep children focused on their building and extend their ideas (Hansel 2017). For example, you might ask:

» What part of the train station are you adding to here? How do the trains get in and out?

» What kind of blocks are you using to build the tower?

» Which blocks are best for building strong walls? How did you find that out?

### As Children Are Representing Their Structures

Drawing their structures helps children become careful observers and strengthens their visual-spatial and small motor skills. Put clipboards with unlined paper and markers in the block area to invite children to draw what they have built or to plan out what they would like to build. Children with language delays or who are dual language learners often communicate what they know through their drawings before they have the ability to verbalize that knowledge. Be sure to encourage them to express what they are thinking. This helps to uncover misconceptions children might have.

Here are some questions you might ask or comments you might make while children draw their structures:

» What part would you like to draw first? (If children are frustrated when trying to draw their block structures, you might help them break the task into steps by starting with this question.)

» What shapes did you use in your drawing of your train station? Are those shapes in the train station you built? Where?

» You said you made a tunnel so the trains can get into the building. Tell me more about that.

## During Group Discussions

Knowing how to ask good questions is challenging, but knowing how to nurture children's curiosity and encourage them to confidently ask their own questions during group discussions can be even more challenging! One strategy is to make reflection an important part of the day. When you create a classroom culture where children learn to listen to one another respectfully in a whole group setting, it helps everyone feel safe and valued. For example, when Luciana completes her train station, Ms. DaNita invites her to share

the drawing she made of the train station with her classmates at group time. The teacher models for the children what it means to show respect for Luciana by looking at her, being quiet when she speaks, and asking her thoughtful questions. Ms. DaNita records important questions and observations the children make on chart paper, clarifying the difference between making an observation and asking a question, and then posts them in the block area. She gently reminds some children not to interrupt when Luciana is speaking and explains that it is an important responsibility of group members to appreciate and acknowledge others' contributions and to give everyone a turn to speak. Engaging children in reflection helps them become more aware of their thinking and what they have learned.

Questions you might ask a child who is sharing her ideas:

» What do you want people to know about your construction?

» What was the most difficult part about creating your _____?

» What did you do about it?

Questions that might arise during group discussion and reflection:

» How did you make the _____?

» Was that hard for you to make? Why or why not?

» How could you make your _____ better or different?

When children plan, construct, and represent their experiences with blocks, they progress in many areas of development and learning (Hansel 2015). You can take what children learn to an even higher level when you ask open-ended questions that encourage children to become more deeply engaged, persist a bit longer, think more creatively, solve challenging problems, collaborate with others, communicate what they know, and apply what they learn to new situations—critical skills that will help children thrive in early childhood and beyond.

### The Picture Book Connection

*Building a House,* by Byron Barton

*Dreaming Up: A Celebration of Building,* by Christy Hale

*The Lot at the End of My Block,* by Kevin Lewis, illustrated by Reg Cartwright

*Roberto: The Insect Architect,* by Nina Laden

*When I Build With Blocks,* by Niki Alling

# Expand Children's Thinking and Learning by Asking Questions

## 1 Remember
(identify, name, count, repeat, recall)

- What shape is your block hotel?
- How many blocks are in your tower?
- Who lives in your building?

## 2 Understand
(describe, discuss, explain, summarize)

- What patterns did you make with your blocks?
- I noticed you put the heavier blocks on the bottom. Why?
- I see your building is different from the drawing you made while planning it. Why did you change your building?

## 3 Apply
(explain why, dramatize, identify with/relate to)

- Use your body to show me how the animals get in and out of the barn.
- How were you able to get the shape to stand up that way?
- How did you get the roof to stay on? Show me how.

## 4 Analyze
(recognize change, experiment, infer, compare, contrast)

- How is your building different from the one Lucas built (from the one in the photos we looked at earlier)?
- What are some other ways to keep the bridge from falling down?
- Which blocks are you going to use for building the castle? Why?

## 5 Evaluate
(express opinion, judge, defend/criticize)

- Which part of your bridge was the trickiest to build? Why?
- What do you think would happen if we took this block out to make a doorway?
- Which blocks make the most interesting buildings? Why do you think so?

## 6 Create
(make, construct, design, author)

- How will you create your skyscraper on paper? What will you write so you'll remember it when we put the blocks away?
- You said that it is very hard to figure out where to put the blocks at cleanup time. How can we make it easier?
- You said that the garage you built is too small to hold all the cars. How can you create a garage that is big enough to fit them all?

The word *mathematics* makes many adults think of rote procedures for getting correct answers, a holdover from our own school days. But, mathematics is essentially the search for sense and meaning, patterns and relationships, order and predictability.

—Juanita V. Copley, *The Young Child and Mathematics,* Second Edition

# Mathematics/ Manipulatives Area

Cindy Gennarelli and Mary DeBlasio

"Good morning, friends!" Ms. Maria greets the children as she enters her preschool classroom. "Kira, today you are the first child to come into the room!" she says while holding up one finger. "Good morning, Jack, you are the second child." This time, Ms. Maria holds up two fingers. She continues to address the children and makes references to the third through the fifteenth as each one arrives.

Each child stops to answer the question of the day that is posted on the whiteboard: How many rocks are in the last jar? There are three jars next to the whiteboard. The first jar has 3 rocks with the number 3 under it, the second has 10 rocks with the number 10, and the third jar has 8 rocks with no number written underneath the jar. As children record their findings on the whiteboard chart, Ms. Maria notes their responses by asking some of the children, "Why did you choose that number?"

At the end of their morning meeting, Ms. Maria reads *Rhoda's Rock Hunt*, by Molly Beth Griffin, and shows the children Rhoda's collection of rocks. She gives each child several small stones and asks what they can tell her about their rocks. The children use words like *smooth, bumpy, big, little, rough*, and *round* to describe their rocks.

As the children choose their interest areas, Ms. Maria reminds them that they have many of the same materials Rhoda played with in the story. "Rhoda sorted, classified, and counted her rocks. I wonder what we can do with ours."

As the children work with the rocks in the mathematics/manipulatives area, she hears comments like "Ms. Maria, look, I just made a pattern!" and "I balanced the rocks."

She responds to each child with comments such as "I see the wonderful pattern you created! Do you think you could make a different pattern with the same rocks?" and "Yes, I see that you balanced the rocks by stacking them on top of each other. I wonder if you could add another."

Ms. Maria notices that two children have created their own question ("Do you like rocks?") using the question graphs that are posted in the mathematics/

manipulatives area as a model. They walk around the classroom surveying their peers with their graph on a clipboard. Both children eagerly remind their friends that they have to make a tally mark in either the yes or the no column.

Kira adds, "Remember, you have to make an up-and-down line. That's a vertical line. But if you count one, two, three, and four vertical lines, then you make a diagonal line. That means you have five."

Later, Ms. Maria asks the two children to tell the class about the results of their survey and what they learned.

Children are born learners who are naturally interested in math, which is part of their everyday experiences. They're very aware of math concepts that are important to them: their age, who had a toy first, who is first in line, or who is faster, taller, or shorter. Yet, they may not have the knowledge or vocabulary to connect what they know to math concepts. It is the teacher's responsibility to develop those connections.

It's easy to use everyday experiences and questioning techniques to foster math vocabulary and develop math concepts, as seen in the brief snapshot of Ms. Maria's classroom. Although it appears that her conversations and activities just happen, she has intentionally chosen not just materials but also the ways that she will make connections between her students' experiences and math. As she greets the children, for example, she refers to ordinal math concepts (noting which child comes in first, second, third, and so on). She uses her fingers to demonstrate number sense. Her questions and suggestions challenge the children to think about the materials they are using, how they're using them, and what their actions result in. The children are excited to participate and respond to the question of the day, which requires them to estimate, count, and write numerals. During center time, she continues to promote math learning with child-centered activities like patterning and balancing and extends their thinking with thoughtful questions and observations.

## Getting Started

Provide math materials that give children opportunities to count, measure, sort, sequence, compare quantities and sizes, recognize shapes and patterns, become familiar with written numbers, and understand time. The materials should include things that children can relate to from their home environment, natural materials, and objects that are new to them. In addition, throughout your classroom, include materials that inspire and promote curiosity, discussion, problem solving, and mathematical learning. Here are some suggestions for materials.

» **Counting:** rocks, sticks, acorns, buttons, bottle caps, pom-poms, beads

» **Measuring:** scales and balances, rulers, measuring tapes, measuring spoons and cups, nonstandard tools like pieces of string, a shoe, a cardboard tracing of a child's hand, or unit blocks

» **Sorting:** items of various colors, sizes, weights, etc., and containers for sorting, such as small recycled cartons and boxes, plastic cups, muffin tins, and ice cube trays

- » **Sequencing/patterning:** shells, leaves, paint color samples, patterning cards depicting items in simple and complex patterns

- » **Comparing quantities and sizes:** manipulatives like dominoes, dot cards, peg number boards, number/quantity puzzles, dice, numeral cards with clothespins for attaching the correct amount

- » **Recognizing shapes and patterns:** pattern block mats and cards, Magna-Tiles, geoboards, shape sorters

- » **Becoming familiar with written numbers:** numerals to trace, magnetic numerals, cash registers, old phones, calendars, birthday charts, recipe cards

- » **Understanding time:** clocks, timers, hourglasses

As children use these items and you ask high-level questions (such as "How can we sort the buttons in a different way?" or "How can we figure out how to make sure the water in the table is just the right height for playing with the small toys?"), children will engage in much more meaningful math learning than if you ask questions like "How many buttons are there?" or "Does this toy float or sink?" Always remember to match the question to a child's developmental level when you are working with individual children. When working with a group, as long as one or more children are ready for a higher-level question, you can scaffold learning for the others.

## Supporting Children's Learning

Helping children build a solid foundation in math is critical to their future success, not only in school, but in their everyday life. Think about whether you give children daily opportunities to be problem solvers, use mathematical vocabulary, reason, and make choices and connections. Here are some ways you can do this:

» Place a balance scale in the water or sand table. While interacting with children, ask questions that encourage them to predict the outcome of their actions: "How many scoops of water (sand) do you need to add to each side of the balance so that both sides are equal?," "What materials from other areas of the room could you add to one side of the scale to balance it with the other?," "Can you combine different materials to balance the scale? If so, what does that mean?"

» Using Unifix cubes as a nonstandard form of measurement, invite the children to measure how tall or long different objects are. Ask them to record their findings. For example, how many Unifix cubes tall is the chair? How many Unifix cubes long is the table? Make a class book about tall and short objects or big and small objects and include drawings, photos, and writing.

» Make cleanup time in the math/manipulatives area a sorting or sequencing experience. When children have mixed different manipulatives together, similar to the activity in the opening vignette of Chapter 1, place all the appropriate labeled storage containers on the table and invite children to sort and classify the materials as they put them away. Ask, "What do you notice about the mixed-up toys in the bowl as you take them out?" For children who are not yet ready for such a high-level question, ask something like "Which trays have the most (least) number of materials?" or "How many cars did you take out?"

» Take a nature walk outdoors and encourage children to look for patterns in nature (McLennan 2017). Bring magnifying glasses, some clipboards, and pencils and ask them to copy the patterns they notice in rocks, spiderwebs, flowers, or other natural objects. Photograph the patterns. Ask children to describe the patterns and talk about whether they think the pattern might change in any way. If you don't have access to these things outdoors, bring them into your classroom.

» Measure the circumference of a pumpkin, tree, or any round object that interests the children (McLennan 2017). Ask them what types of standard and nonstandard tools they might use to do that. Don't be afraid to use and explain sophisticated words like *circumference*.

» Take an old checkerboard and some loose parts (dice, spinners, etc.) and invite the children to create a board game (McLennan 2017). Or, draw a large checkerboard on a blacktop area outdoors and have children create a large motor board game! Ask, "How can we use this board and these pieces to make a game that we can play?" or "How can we move our bodies around on these chalk drawings so that we are pieces in the game?"

### The Picture Book Connection

*Balancing Act*, by Ellen Stoll Walsh

*Ernest, the Moose Who Doesn't Fit*, by Catherine Rayner

*Perfect Square*, by Michael Hall

*Shapes That Roll*, by Karen Nagel, illustrated by Steve Wilson

*You Are (Not) Small*, by Anna Kang, illustrated by Christopher Weyant

# Expand Children's Thinking and Learning by Asking Questions

**1** **Remember**
(identify, name, count, repeat, recall)

- How many people live in your house?
- What is this shape called?
- How many puzzle pieces are in this police station puzzle?

**2** **Understand**
(describe, discuss, explain, summarize)

- Tell me about the pattern you made with the beads on your string.
- What kind of shapes will you use in your collage?
- Explain how you will figure out how many children are here today.

**3** **Apply**
(explain why, dramatize, identify with/relate to)

- Use the five stick puppets of ducks to sing and act out "Five Little Ducks."
- How can we make sure that everyone gets a cookie if we only have 10 cookies and we have 12 children in our class today?
- How can you make a square (circle, rectangle, triangle) with your whole body (hands, feet) by yourself (with one other person, with several other people)?

**4** **Analyze**
(recognize change, experiment, infer, compare, contrast)

- How is the pattern Manuel made with the blocks different from (the same as) yours?
- How can we find out whose plant grew the most while we were on vacation?
- How would the classroom look different to you if you were really tall (short)? Let's experiment.

**5** **Evaluate**
(express opinion, judge, defend/criticize)

- Which materials would make a really interesting pattern?
- Using the balance scale, what would you need to add to each side to make the balance level?
- Which would be the best material for measuring how long the block area carpet is? Why?

**6** **Create**
(make, construct, design, author)

- What will you draw (photograph, glue) on each page of the number book you are making?
- Since the crib in the dramatic play area is too small for this new baby doll, how could you make one that she can fit in? What's your plan for designing it?
- How can you combine these pattern blocks to create a new shape (design)?

Engineering stimulates the mind. Kids get bored easily. They have got to get out and get their hands dirty: make things, dismantle things, fix things. When schools can offer that, you'll have an engineer for life.

—Bruce Dickinson, "Iron Maiden's Bruce Dickinson on His Airline Ambitions," interview with Russell Hotten for BBC News

# A Makerspace in the Science Area

**Megan King**

Dashawn, Kaylie, and Avery, a group of 3- and 4-year-old children in my class, look through a book about hot air balloons.

**Dashawn:** Ms. King, why does it have to be hot air in the balloon?

**Ms. King:** I'm not sure. I wonder how we could figure that out.

**Dashawn:** (after thinking a moment) Can we try putting cold air in instead?

**Ms. King:** Maybe you can design an experiment to test that theory.

Dashawn, Kaylie, and Avery move to the makerspace in the science area and begin to brainstorm the design of their experiment. After several minutes, the children return with drawings of their "cold air" balloon designs.

**Ms. King:** Explain your experiments to me.

**Dashawn:** I'm putting the ice cubes in the balloon, and then it will go down because the hot air balloon goes up.

**Kaylie:** Mine is full of water, cold water. It will go down, too.

**Avery:** I want to put snow in mine, but it's not time for snow.

You may question whether 3- and 4-year-old children could really initiate such inquiry. If teachers redefine their thinking about science in the classroom and offer thought-provoking materials and experiences, they can. Although some young children and their teachers don't usually use sophisticated words like *experiment* and *theory,* when you regularly use more challenging words and phrases in the context of children's activities, they become a part of their vocabularies. Try it, and you'll be amazed! Because the children in my classroom have had adult support and opportunities to conduct experiments to find out the answers to their questions, they readily engage in hypothesizing, brainstorming, experimenting, and problem solving.

Teachers often get caught up in "magic show" science that is typically done with preschoolers—like mixing baking soda and vinegar to simulate a volcano eruption and then asking children to describe what they see. Although children look at these displays with wonder and amazement, do these activities really contribute to the development of their inquiry skills? While there is some validity in activities like these, the problem is that some teachers stop there. They test children's recall skills, but they stop short of encouraging children to ask their own questions, create, test their theories, and really ponder what they're experiencing.

How do you move toward a classroom culture that encourages children to consider and ask thought-provoking questions? The key is redefining what you think of as science.

## Getting Started

Think of a typical science area in an early childhood classroom. What items are you most likely to see? A collection of shells, leaves, and rocks; magnetic wands; magnifying glasses; plants; and a fish tank. These basic materials have framed the way you may look at science but do these objects actually encourage children to think and develop their own questions about the world around them?

While these items may be enticing at the beginning of the school year, by the time November rolls around, the children are finished exploring them and are ready for something new. As the children's interest in the materials fades, their opportunities to practice critical thinking, problem solving, predicting, and concluding also fade; as a result, the science area becomes one of the least used areas of the classroom (see Chapter 11 for a discussion of natural science as part of outdoor learning). Young learners can't be expected to develop the skills they need to understand, apply, analyze, evaluate, and create unless teachers provide opportunities for them to be curious and deepen their learning beyond remembering. To get young children to the point where they can consider, answer, and even ask their own high-level questions, you need to put more open-ended materials in their hands—materials that will stimulate curiosity and exploration.

One way to do this is to transform your science area into a makerspace. The maker movement, which started in the technology world, has since spread into education and is revolutionizing the way teachers think about what students can do and learn. A makerspace is a place where people come together to work on projects. Its primary purpose is to provide opportunities for *making*—using shared resources to create. You may have seen a makerspace at your local or school library, a mixture of high- and low-tech gadgets, art projects, computer coding programs, sewing machines, and table saws. With some modifications, this concept can be applied to early childhood as well. It simply requires the addition of materials that encourage creativity, imagination, exploration, and inquiry along with adults who encourage a "What can we create?" mindset. By replacing high-tech gadgets with old and/or broken VCRs and radios, for example, children can explore and tinker with their inner workings, developing the skills necessary to understand and question their world. Substituting fabric scraps and blunt plastic sewing needles for sewing machines gives children the opportunity to practice problem solving and create new garments for the classroom. The inclusion of these items, coupled with questions or

comments that are designed to encourage children to apply, evaluate, create, and take risks will ultimately support the higher-level thinking skills necessary for children to thrive in our changing world.

Makerspaces are one of the most progressive additions to preschool and kindergarten classrooms in recent years. As new technologies are developed and twenty-first century skills have moved to the forefront of education, teachers have been called on to prepare students for an ever-changing future. By adding a makerspace to your science area, you are providing hands-on opportunities for children to interact with scientific concepts by problem solving, experimenting, and creating things that make abstract concepts more tangible.

You may be asking, "What materials could possibly do all this for a young child, and where can I get my hands on them?" The good news is many of them already exist in your classroom and the others are easy enough to come by to get started. In creating this space for children, consider that it should facilitate learning in a safe, developmentally appropriate way. The materials could include large marbles, LEGO bricks, KEVA planks, Snap Circuits, items to build simple machines, real child-size tools, test tubes, small motors, and mini robots. These are just some examples of the kinds of materials that encourage children to solve problems, experiment, develop theories, test their ideas, and create new uses for everyday resources.

## Supporting Children's Learning

As children work with these materials, there are ample opportunities to build on their knowledge, ask questions, and encourage them to ask their own questions. When children play and work with open-ended materials like these, they are challenged and stimulated to try to solve the problems they encounter. Asking children questions during these exploratory moments supports the development of abstract thinking. When working with lengths of PVC pipe and connector pieces, wooden blocks, and marbles to construct a marble run, a child might encounter a problem. A good question might be, "Why do you think the marble isn't going down through your structure?" Younger learners might not be able to answer this type of question, but you may get them thinking about how they can evaluate the situation. With appropriate interactions, the child may soon be ready to take on such questions and even begin to ask them herself.

You can also develop lessons based on how children use materials or based on a problem children encounter in their play. For example, a group of children was working with a simple machines building kit, experimenting specifically with the lever. After observing this, the teacher planned a small group lesson on building a lever to toss cotton balls. Children were given plastic cups in various sizes, craft sticks, bottle caps, tape, glue, rubber bands, and unit, pillar, ramp, and cylinder blocks to attempt to construct a lever that would toss the cotton ball the farthest. As the children experimented with angles, heights, and weights, the teacher asked them questions at various levels to support their learning. She asked about the materials they were using, how they were using them, what was different about throwing cotton balls by hand and using the lever to launch them, what they could tell her about how the cotton balls traveled, why they thought the lever made the cotton balls travel farther, and how they might use a lever in the block area.

You don't need to completely redefine your science area all at once. Consider starting with a tinkering box made with found materials and inexpensive items from a trip to a dollar store. A well-equipped collection might contain screwdrivers, screws, springs, nuts, bolts, tape (masking, duct, electrical), hammers, nails, twine, sandpaper, wood scraps, glue, rubber bands, boxes, measuring tapes, rulers, wire, empty plastic bottles, bottle caps, and corks. Little by little, your science area will turn into an exciting makerspace!

## The Picture Book Connection

*If I Built a House,* by Chris Van Dusen

*The Most Magnificent Thing,* by Ashley Spires

*Robots, Robots Everywhere!* by Sue Fliess

*The Three Little Pigs: An Architectural Tale,* by Steven Guarnaccia

*Violet the Pilot,* by Steve Breen

### More Resources on Makerspaces

Brahms, L., & P.S. Wardrip. 2017. "The What, How, and Why of Making." *Teaching Young Children* 10 (3): 16–17.

Bresson, L.M., & M. King. 2017. "Inventions, Gizmos, and Gadgets—Oh My! How to Help Your Preschoolers Get the Most Out of Your Makerspace." *Teaching Young Children* 10 (2): 24–26.

Heroman, C. 2017. *Making and Tinkering With STEM: Solving Design Challenges With Young Children.* Washington, DC: NAEYC.

# Expand Children's Thinking and Learning by Asking Questions

**1** **Remember**
(identify, name, count, repeat, recall)

- What material(s) are you using?
- How many planks are you stacking?
- Which screws are longer (shorter) than the one you're using?

**2** **Understand**
(describe, discuss, explain, summarize)

- Tell me how you're using the planks.
- What happens when you drop the marble in?
- How did you fix the flashlight?

**3** **Apply**
(explain why, dramatize, identify with/relate to)

- Where else have you seen this liquid?
- Show me with your hands what would happen if the tube for the marbles went side to side instead of up and down.
- Why do you think the plant leaves turned brown?

**4** **Analyze**
(recognize change, experiment, infer, compare, contrast)

- What happened when you mixed the oil and water?
- Which material worked better in this experiment?
- Why is the AA battery giving the robot more power than the button cell battery?

**5** **Evaluate**
(express opinion, judge, defend/criticize)

- Why did the marble get stuck?
- What are some reasons your machine worked (didn't work)?
- Why do you think that would be the best tool to tighten the screws on your machine?

**6** **Create**
(make, construct, design, author)

- How will you make a complete circuit?
- What kind of maze can you create for the robot?
- How will you write (draw) the directions to explain how you made the hot air balloon?

Preschoolers need writing to help them learn about reading and reading to help them learn about writing. They need to talk and listen to help them learn about both.

—Kathleen A. Roskos, James F. Christie, and Donald J. Richgels, "Reading, Writing, and Talking: Strategies for Preschool Classrooms," *Learning About Language and Literacy in Preschool*

# Writing Area

**5**

Kathleen Whalen

During an exploration of color and light in an urban preschool classroom of 4-year-olds, two children, Abraham and Brielle, gather around the art table. They are creating various shades of blue by mixing blue, black, and white tempera paint in muffin tins.

Abraham exclaims, "I make so many blue colors."

"Me too," replies Brielle, "Mine is so many different kinds of blue. I mix it here with the white and black. Now the colors are different. Some go to dark and darker and darker."

Their teacher, Mr. Kassim, sits down beside the children and observes the problem solving the children are using. Then he comments, "I noticed that you both created darker shades and lighter shades of blue. How did you do that?" Both children eagerly explain their processes.

Mr. Kassim says thoughtfully, "You created many shades of blue. They remind me of the *Pantone: Colors* book we keep in the art area. I wonder if you could name the shades that you created, like in that book."

"Yeah!" says Brielle. "We looked at the book. It has a lot of names." She walks quickly to the art area where there are various books about colors for reference. Brielle opens the book and her teacher points to the writing under the various colors.

"Remember we talked about this book during morning meeting? It names so many shades of color. Why do you think it was important to write the names down?" asks Mr. Kassim.

Abraham answers, "So everyone can know they are special colors."

"I made this color," Brielle says, pointing to her work. "It's called Big Daddy Blue because it's the darkest, darkest one."

"And this one is Itty Bitty Baby Blue because it only has a little blue," says Abraham.

"You could write all of this down," suggests Mr. Kassim. "That way everyone will know the special names of your shades."

Both children spend 20 minutes adding dots of various shades of blue to pieces of paper and carefully writing names for each with Mr. Kassim's assistance. The teacher makes sure to call attention to the children's efforts at the close of center time. He encourages both children to share their writing and reason for writing with their peers.

Opportunities for children to engage in writing can—and should—occur in all interest areas, not just the writing area. When you talk about the importance of writing and connect it to meaningful classroom experiences, children are more motivated and likely to write with both purpose and intention. Building on these opportunities by asking high-level questions will only help to deepen children's engagement.

Although writing should be supported throughout the classroom, creating a designated writing area that is equipped with a variety of writing tools, paper, staplers, paper clips, and additional materials offers children the opportunity to write for various purposes, such as creating greeting cards, sending messages to family members and peers, and writing stories. Carefully designing the physical space also makes it easier to ask high-level questions, as both you and children will have the materials you need at your fingertips.

## Getting Started

Be prepared and intentional in your teaching. Spend some time writing down specific questions you plan to ask ahead of time. These questions can be tied to a specific exploration or general questions that fit into a variety of scenarios. As you are thinking of questions, have handy the list of key skills you want to address. Gear your questions toward each of these skills, and write them down on sticky notes or index cards. Add these notes to your lesson plans or classroom writing area in a way that is not obvious to children. Questions can also be based on your observations in the moment and may arise spontaneously as you interact with children. These teachable moments can and should be harnessed to scaffold learning. Also, learn to comment on children's work by making statements about what you see them doing, followed by an open-ended question or remark.

Next, set a personal goal to ask at least one question or make one observation during a one-to-one interaction with a child. This would also be a good time to reflect on the amount of time you spend with children in small groups as well as individually. Although asking high-level questions is important during group times, you will gain deeper insight into children's thinking as you question children on a more personal level. Create a tracking sheet that allows you to monitor the time you spend with children individually. This will help you to be more intentional with your time and ensure that you are spending a similar amount of time with each child.

Along with planning for questioning, you can create folders for each child. Include drawing and writing samples, examples of dictation, and photos of the children's writing in the folders. Refer to them often, and when you encourage children to add their favorite pieces to their portfolio, give them the opportunity to reflect on their writing process. On the inside flap of the writing folder, record each time you have a one-to-one interaction with the child as well as a question you asked and the child's response. This can also be a great area to record questions you want to ask at a later time, making the class portfolios living documents that continue to grow and change throughout the school year.

## Supporting Children's Learning

For young children, writing means a combination of drawing, writing, and dictating. As children begin to make marks on paper, be sure to encourage their efforts at all levels. Early experiences with writing are about children learning to express their thoughts and understanding the functions and features of print. It is also critical to get down to children's eye level when asking questions and commenting on their writing.

Observe and gather information about children, both individually and as a group. The more information you have, the better you will be able to support their learning and ask questions appropriate for each child's level of development. Document what children say and do in the writing area or as they write in other interest areas in a number of ways. One technique is to record children's dictations, which means writing down exactly what children say as they write or read their writing to you; another is to collect samples of their writing. You might also take photographs of children writing and include a description of what they are working on or what they discussed with you about their process. Your reflections on the documentation and your interactions with children will help decide the types of questions you ask.

## The Picture Book Connection

*Dog Loves Drawing,* by Louise Yates

*The Line,* by Paula Bossio

*A Line Can Be,* by Laura Ljungkvist

*Lines That Wiggle,* by Candace Whitman, illustrated by Steve Wilson

*A Squiggly Story,* by Andrew Larsen, illustrated by Mike Lowery

As previously mentioned, making an observational statement about a child's work *before* you ask a question shows you are genuinely interested in her work and that you have taken the time to truly examine what she is doing. This can be done spontaneously as you interact with the children during their play. For example, you might say something like, "I see that you wrote about going to California with Jaeven. Tell me what you two are going to do next." Simple statements like this both acknowledge what the child has already worked on and encourage her to extend her thinking. Becoming skilled at commenting on children's work is essential as you begin to offer more specific feedback and questions.

# Expand Children's Thinking and Learning by Asking Questions

## 1 Remember
(identify, name, count, repeat, recall)

- What letters did you use in your writing?
- What materials did you use to write your poem (letter, story)?
- What types of lines did you use?

## 2 Understand
(describe, discuss, explain, summarize)

- Tell me about your writing (drawing).
- Where did you begin? Where did you finish?
- Why did you write this letter next to your drawing?

## 3 Apply
(explain why, dramatize, identify with/relate to)

- Why did you write or draw about _____?
- How does this piece of writing make you feel? Why?
- Show us how the waiter in the restaurant read the specials of the day to his customers on the pad where you wrote those items down.

## 4 Analyze
(recognize change, experiment, infer, compare, contrast)

- How has your writing changed since you wrote this last story about your dog?
- Thanks for sharing your thoughts about your drawing with me! I wrote it down here in the corner of the paper. How do you think this will be helpful when other people look at your drawing?
- What happens when you press really hard on the paper with your crayon? And what about when you hold it lightly in your hand and press softly? Which way works best when you try to write?

## 5 Evaluate
(express opinion, judge, defend/criticize)

- What are some reasons this is your favorite piece of writing?
- What do you think is the best tool in the writing area to attach all the pages of your book together? Why?
- These are different kinds of fancy letters you can type with on the computer. They're called *fonts*. Which kind do you like the best? Why?

## 6 Create
(make, construct, design, author)

- How can you create a book that tells a story about your family trip (house, dog, baby brother)?
- How can we invite our families to the art gallery?
- How will you design the menu for your new pizza restaurant?

The questions thus serve as doorways or lenses through which learners can better see and explore the key concepts, themes, theories, issues, and problems that reside within the content.

—Jay McTighe and Grant Wiggins, *Essential Questions: Opening Doors to Student Understanding*

# Art Area

Triada Samaras

Ms. Rivas, an artist in residence at the local community school, sits with a small group of preschool children in front of a collection of recycled materials. She smiles and greets each of them warmly. Some of the students are dual language learners, and they watch her movements intently.

Ms. Rivas picks up a crumpled piece of aluminum foil, pinching it gently between her fingertips. "Do you know the name of this material?" she asks. "Have you seen it before? What is it used for?"

"Aluminum foil! I saw that in my kitchen!" Luis exclaims.

Mateo emphatically replies, "I use it for my tuna fish sandwich, to wrap it in the morning!"

Other students nod in agreement.

"I saw that on a Christmas tree in my country!" Arabella answers. "And it was so beautiful!"

"Wow," Ms. Rivas comments. "That's a lot of things it can be used for! I wonder how *we* can use it."

She gives each child a piece of foil. Mateo takes his piece and rolls it between his palms, while Arabella begins twisting hers around her pointer finger.

Luis holds his piece delicately with his fingertips, watching it shimmer under the overhead lights. "I can glue it on our mural to be stars in the sky."

Ms. Rivas watches as the children explore the foil and chatter excitedly to each other. She knows their classroom teacher has just introduced a study of creative inventions, so she makes a note to bring in a book about mechanical robots next week. While looking through the book with the children, she plans on guiding them with a series of high-level questions to make connections between the inventions they have been studying and the new art materials she has introduced.

Artmaking in the early childhood classroom is much more than putting playdough or tempera paint in the art area. Creating rich classroom experiences that seamlessly integrate art into other content areas and promote high-level thinking involves planning, creating, and reflecting about collaborative artmaking with children (Mufson & Strasser 2016). The best art materials are those children love using, and the best art experiences allow students to use these art materials in ways that are inspired by their ideas.

Exploration is an essential step when introducing new art materials to children. All young children need time to play and experiment freely before you introduce a theme or suggest that they use materials in new ways. During this phase you might make observations like "The paper you have in your hand is really shiny" or "Look what happens to the clay when you push your finger into it."

After observing how children interact with the art materials, determine when and how to introduce a specific theme. Here, you can expand on the exploration stage. Extend your initial observation about the shiny paper by asking, "What are some ways you've seen this shiny material used before? What did you think about that?" Continue a child's line of thinking about the clay you commented on by saying, "Which clay tool do you like the best so far? Why?"

### What Do Children Learn from the Arts?

World-renowned art educator Elliot Eisner established some of the lessons closely aligned with high-level thinking that students learn naturally through the artmaking process (Eisner 2004):

- There isn't just a single answer to a question.
- People view the world differently.
- Art is a nonverbal way of expressing yourself.
- Sometimes little changes can make a big difference.
- Experiencing a work of art can inspire an emotional reaction in children.

Appropriate themes or topics emerge from the children and often include families, neighborhoods, animals, transportation, and inventions. However, there's no need to limit themes to just content. You can study artmaking processes like printmaking, color mixing, and collage for extended periods of time with young children. When you plan a theme- or topic-based artmaking experience, keep it broad and flexible to accommodate and support children's own ideas about using the art materials. This is a natural part of the creative process and an important way to support children's creative thinking.

## Getting Started

Include a variety of open-ended materials that children can take out and put away on their own, including crayons; markers; paper of various sizes, colors, and shapes; tempera paint; clay; playdough; Wikki Stix; wire; papier-mâché; stamps and ink pads; fabrics; yarn; and recycled and natural materials. Open-ended art experiences should include woodworking, mural making, printing, observational drawing, and palette painting. Give children opportunities to work with real clay as well as playdough. Set the stage for creative, individualized artwork with a range of tools, like scissors, tape, hole punchers, staplers, brads, glue, unbreakable mirrors, magnifying glasses, and brushes.

Provide red, yellow, blue, black, and white paints in small, shallow containers, like jar lids. Invite the children to put dabs of colors onto a palette (such as a paper plate) so they can mix them together and create new shades. Have small sponges and cups of water on hand for them to clean their brushes as they make new colors. Teach the children what making a quick sketch means. You can model this with a pencil or crayon and a piece of paper on a clipboard. Pick an object in the classroom (a chair) or outside (a tree), and using the pencil or crayon, show the children how you can make a few simple lines on the paper that mimic the object's basic shape. Then, when you take neighborhood walks or go outside to play, have clipboards and pencils available for children to sketch anything that catches their interest—birds, trees, cars, or the skyline.

Introduce young children to famous artists and work across an extensive spectrum of techniques and styles to study and compare their work. A few suggestions include realist (Chuck Close), impressionist (Claude Monet), abstract (Wassily Kandinsky), surrealist (Salvador Dalí), and pop (Andy Warhol).

## Supporting Children's Exploration and Learning

Support children's artistic, creative, and critical thinking skills by using intentional questioning strategies. You can ask questions before, during, and after any art experience (see the examples on page 46). When you sit with the children at the art table to talk about their projects, before they start using materials, focus on questions that are likely to motivate them. While children are working with the art materials, ask questions about how the children are exploring the materials, topic, or theme. Once they are finished,

the children can gather in small or large groups to study each other's works, either with or without you. Instead of saying "That's beautiful!" or "I love your painting!," you can say, "The combination of those two colors is really nice for me to look at. It reminds me of . . ." or "I can tell you put a lot work into this. All of these details show me you were concentrating on your sculpture for a long time!" Focus on each child's unique creation and ask specific questions related to the artwork and process.

Questions to ask **before** artmaking:

- » How could you use this material in your creation?
- » What other materials would be interesting to combine with this one?
- » What colors (shapes, patterns, lines) are you thinking about using for your creation?
- » What does this material make you think about?

Questions to ask **during** artmaking:

- » How did you draw these wiggly lines (different colored forms)?
- » Can you pretend to draw this shape in the air with your hand?
- » How could you use this recycled material to create the shapes, forms, and textures in a different way?

Questions to ask **after** artmaking:

- » What is your favorite part of this artwork? Why?
- » What kinds of textures (lines, shapes, colors, forms) did you use? Where do you see them?
- » How did you make such a tall creation, and how did you make it balance?
- » What were you thinking about while you invented this artwork?
- » How does this artwork make you feel?

Artmaking involves a creative combination of open-ended materials and tools alongside thoughtful encouragement from adults. When you incorporate the elements of art, the principles of design, *and* ask high-level questions, children learn to be creative thinkers as they make unique, complex works of art!

## The Picture Book Connection

*Harold and the Purple Crayon,* by Crockett Johnson

*Matthew's Dream,* by Leo Lionni

*Papa's Mechanical Fish,* by Candace Fleming, illustrated by Boris Kulikov

*Press Here,* by Hervé Tullet

*What Do You Do With an Idea?* by Kobi Yamada, illustrated by Mae Besom

# Expand Children's Thinking and Learning by Asking Questions

**1**   **Remember**
(identify, name, count, repeat, recall)

- What shapes did you use to print with yesterday?
- What are the names of these materials in our collage box?
- What colors did you use in your painting?

**2**   **Understand**
(describe, discuss, explain, summarize)

- Describe how this material looks (feels, sounds).
- Explain how you made purple for your painting when you started with only red, yellow, blue, black, and white paints.
- How did you fit all of these shapes on top of your sculpture?

**3**   **Apply**
(explain why, dramatize, identify with/relate to)

- In what kind of building might you see this material?
- If you could live somewhere in this artwork, where would it be and why?
- Can you make the same sound as this material when I crunch it all up? How?

**4**   **Analyze**
(recognize change, experiment, infer, compare, contrast)

- How is the tissue paper the same as the construction paper you used, and how are they different?
- What do you think might happen if you made your sculpture taller (shorter)?
- Bella and Charlie, how would you compare the paintings you each did of your families?

**5**   **Evaluate**
(express opinion, judge, defend/criticize)

- What parts of your artwork are your least favorite? Why?
- Which part of your mural are you most proud of? Why?
- Which of these famous artists do you think has the most interesting style—Van Gogh, Picasso, or Pollock? Why?

**6**   **Create**
(make, construct, design, author)

- What type of artwork are you interested in creating for the cover of your *All About Me* book?
- How will you begin your family collage?
- What should we title our mural about our families?

# Using Questions
# During Other Parts
# of the Daily Routine

Class meetings help create a safe environment for everyone. [They] can transform a group of individual children into a real community of learners.

—Emily Vance, *Class Meetings: Young Children Solving Problems Together*, Revised Edition

# Class Meetings

Today is Hermia's turn to ring the bell and convene the class meeting. She knows she is supposed to sing "Come to the rug, now! Come to the rug, now!" to gather the students, but she is feeling shy and asks her friend Maryluz to help her. They giggle and sing it together.

As the children come to the rug, Hermia pauses to make positive comments the way Mrs. McCombs has modeled for her kindergarten students. "Lanae, thanks for cleaning up the block area so fast. Jonah, I saw you help Trevon tie his shoe. That was very kind!"

Once everyone is sitting on the rug, she tells Mrs. McCombs that the class is ready to start their meeting. Mrs. McCombs acknowledges the thoughtful comments Hermia made to the children as they gathered and notes how pleased she was to hear that Jonah helped Trevon tie his shoe. Next, as the convener, Hermia chooses the song they'll use to start their meeting. From the picture prompts on the interactive whiteboard, she chooses "Today Is Monday." She presses the prompt and the words come onto the screen. After they sing, Hermia counts the students that are present, and puts an *x* on the whiteboard next to the name of the student who is absent.

Mrs. McCombs asks, "Who has something that they would like to share?" The children know that they can talk about something exciting that happened in school, something they are sad or worried about, a problem they're having, or any general observation.

Dunia shouts happily, "Maryluz said she liked my LEGO creation!"

"I finished the whole 50-piece puzzle by myself for the first time!" James calls out.

Trevon raises his hand and says, "Jonah didn't let me work on the animal hospital class book with him in the writing area."

"So, not having a chance to work together on the book was upsetting for you," Mrs. McCombs replies. She asks the class to think-pair-share ideas about how to handle a situation where one person wants to do something alone and another wants to work together. After two or three minutes, she asks them to share some of their ideas, which include, "Sometimes, you just feel like writing by yourself, so the other person should just go and make their own page," "Maybe Jonah was mad about something," and "Trevon could come and help me with my block building of the animal doctor." Mrs. McCombs asks Trevon if any of these ideas are things he might try if something like this happens again. Trevon nods and says, "Yeah, I could just make my own picture and then staple it in the book later."

Mrs. McCombs goes over the schedule for the day, and then Hermia chooses the song "Goodbye Everybody, Yes Indeed" to end the meeting. The teacher thanks everyone for sharing and helping the class become a caring community. Hermia calls on her classmates one by one, and each child takes a turn selecting the interest area they will work in that morning.

Class meetings serve many purposes. You may bring a group of children together to take care of daily tasks like announcements, give them information like what to do during a fire drill, or review something they recently learned. Some of these discussions center on lower-level questions like these: "What should you do when the fire alarm goes off?" or "What number comes after 12?" Class meetings are also times when children can solve problems and work together creatively. Using high-level questions during these meetings is a great way to promote a sense of community, support social and emotional growth, and enhance learning and literacy.

## Getting Started

Stick to a time frame for class meetings that is developmentally appropriate for the children you work with. For preschoolers, this is usually 5 minutes at the beginning of the school year with a gradual buildup to 15 minutes, depending on their developmental level and individual needs. Kindergarten meetings can be a bit longer if the children are engaged, but it should not exceed 20 minutes. Even if it seems brief to you, the best way to judge whether a meeting is too long is to take your cue from the children. If you are discussing a problem that affects the group, or a serious issue like bullying, realize that *many* discussions will be needed over time to help children sort through the issue and figure out potential solutions.

### A Space to Talk Through Problems

When you invite children to discuss problems, encourage them to come up with solutions rather than blame, punish, or make negative comments about anyone. Asking high-level questions like "What is one way both you and José could have a chance to use the tablet today?" and "How do you think this situation would have turned out differently if you hadn't grabbed the tablet from José's hands? Let's role-play some other ways we could solve the problem." Remember that "not all problems need to be solved. Sometimes children just need to talk about a situation and have their feelings acknowledged. Children need to be heard" (Vance 2014, 27).

It's important to never pressure a child to attend a class meeting. Some children need more time than others to feel comfortable talking and listening in a large group setting, particularly when the focus is on problems. They should be permitted to quietly do something else (like work on a puzzle or draw) until they are ready to join. In some cases, this may take a week or two. Even though they are not sitting with the group, the child can still listen and think about what is being said.

In addition to high-level questions, active listening strategies are extremely important. When children speak,

remember to give them your complete attention, make them feel comfortable sharing, reflect on what they say, and summarize their comments. This is precisely what Mrs. McCombs did in her response to Trevon's problem with Jonah in the writing area.

Class meetings can be one of the most special and rewarding times of the day as adults and children explore high-level thinking to grow as individuals and as a caring community.

## Supporting Children's Learning

Class meetings should follow a framework that consists of opening, acknowledgments, problem solving, and closing (Vance 2014). Within this framework, you can make class meetings unique and engaging by creating your own routines and traditions. The meetings should be held at the same time each day, and openings and closings should follow a routine so that children know what is expected. In Mrs. McCombs's class, each student gets a turn to convene the daily meeting. She also uses a song to begin and end the meeting, while other teachers may use poems, fingerplays, or brief large motor activities (like movements to the song "Head, Shoulders, Knees, and Toes"). The opening and closing components of class meetings let children enter the group at their own pace and exit the group with a feeling of closure and very little direction from the teacher.

Initially, acknowledgments can start with your comments on specific positive behaviors you have noticed the class participating in. You might offer examples of children sharing, cooperating, and being kind to one another. Instead of generalized praise ("Elena had good behavior today," and "Vrishak did a good job at lunchtime"), use statements that describe specific accomplishments, such as "Elena remembered to use her words when someone knocked over her puzzle," and "Vrishak helped clean up all of the juice that spilled."

When there is a positive social climate in the classroom, the group can discuss problems openly and without judgment. Just as Mrs. McCombs reminded Trevon and Jonah of a positive interaction they had that day, you can draw attention to the fact that even though classmates experience problems sometimes, they are still part of a community and everyone is accepted.

After a while, children will begin to share acknowledgments as well. High-level questions come into play here as you ask children to reflect on the positive things that are going on. As they analyze (Level 4) and evaluate (Level 5) the positive social and emotional behaviors they see occurring, they will begin to recognize change ("Marlon is sharing the crayons now") or express their opinions ("Aaron didn't cry when he had to wait a long time to have a turn at the workbench").

The main component of the class meeting is usually problem solving. Sometimes there are problems that you notice, such as two children having difficulty getting along, someone getting bullied, or materials not being put away properly. Other times, children may share something personal, like an illness in the family or being mad at a sibling. If no one has anything to share, use this time to reflect on children's social and emotional growth by asking questions that help them think about changes that have taken place or things they're working on, like "What have you noticed about the way we are working on getting along with our friends?" or "How can we change the way we come to the rug for story time so that everyone gets a chance to sit in the front sometimes?" This time can also be used to brainstorm about an upcoming class project or event, such as how to start a vegetable garden in the courtyard, how to decide what kind of class pet to get, or how to share with the rest of the school some of the things they learned from their class visit to the veterinary hospital. Whatever the content of your class meetings, think about ways you can use questions and comments to encourage children to think in more complex ways about challenges, relationships, and learning.

## The Picture Book Connection

*The Boy Who Wouldn't Share,* by Mike Reiss, illustrated by David Catrow

*Bully,* by Laura Vaccaro Seeger

*Hey, Little Ant,* by Phillip and Hannah Hoose, illustrated by Debbie Tilley

*My New Friend Is So Fun!* by Mo Willems

*Sometimes I'm Bombaloo,* by Rachel Vail, illustrated by Yumi Heo

# Expand Children's Thinking and Learning by Asking Questions

## 1 Remember
(identify, name, count, repeat, recall)

- How many students are wearing blue pants today?
- Who is not here today?
- What are we going to do after lunch?

## 2 Understand
(describe, discuss, explain, summarize)

- How do you think our new pet guinea pig is feeling in her new surroundings?
- How does the class rule "use your listening ears" help us be good community members?
- What did you do to help Alexa feel better after her feelings were hurt?

## 3 Apply
(explain why, dramatize, identify with/relate to)

- Why do you think Gabe got upset when he couldn't open the paint container?
- If you worked really hard at making a roller coaster with the materials in the makerspace and someone knocked it over and it fell apart, what would you do?
- We talked about McKenzie feeling worried when her dad had to stay in the hospital for a few days. Can you share a time when you felt worried? What did you do?

## 4 Analyze
(recognize change, experiment, infer, compare, contrast)

- Think about the way we set up the obstacle course outside. What's working well? How could we change it to make it more challenging or fun?
- What can we change about the way we clean up that will help us put the blocks away in the right places?
- How will we change the way we take care of our parakeet after our visit to the veterinary hospital?

## 5 Evaluate
(express opinion, judge, defend/criticize)

- What can Kayla do to make Harper feel better after what happened on the playground today?
- In the book *Hey, Little Ant*, do you think it's okay for the boy to step on the ant? Why or why not?
- What do you think about the display we made to tell the rest of the school about our catapult project? Do you think it's effective? Why or why not?

## 6 Create
(make, construct, design, author)

- If you created a sign that had a message to bullies, what would it look like and what would it say?
- Sometimes we get really angry. What ideas can we include in this basket (on this list) that can help us stay calm when we need it?
- What can we draw on our class mural to show all the great things we do to help each other in Room 2?

Guiding a good discussion after a story reading deepens the basic understanding that children have built *during* a story.

—Judith A. Schickedanz and Molly F. Collins, *So Much More than the ABCs: The Early Phases of Reading and Writing*

# Read-Alouds

8

Holly Seplocha

It's a perfect April day with blue skies, white fluffy clouds, and a little breeze. Ms. Jordan decides to take her class of 4-year-olds outside and have a read-aloud after large motor play. When playground time is over, she calls the children back and asks them sit in a circle, lie on their backs in the grass, and look up at the sky.

"What do you see?" she asks, and children respond with things like "Sky," "A bird," and "The sun is hiding." She then invites the children to sit up as she reads *Little Cloud*, by Eric Carle.

After reading the book, she tells the children to lie down again. "See if you can find your own little cloud in the sky. What does it look like?" Pausing to allow for some answers, she tells them to close their eyes and count to 10 with her. "Now open your eyes. Can you find your little cloud from before? What does your little cloud look like now?"

They repeat this activity two more times before sitting up. Ms. Jordan recalls some of the answers and then asks, "Why do you think your little cloud changed shape so many times?"

"'Cause there's lots of wind," replies Irina.

"When the birds fly," adds Daan, "maybe they move the clouds around."

Ms. Jordan says, "When we go inside, I've set up a big sky-colored paper on the art table. What materials could you use to make some little clouds?"

Reading aloud opens the door to learning, giving children a special kind of access to the power of story and the experience of what reading is all about. Asking questions during read-alouds fosters opportunities for children to discuss big ideas about themselves, the lives of others, and their world. When you read to children, you free them to think about a choice a character made, how the book relates to their own experiences, and the concept or topic the book addresses. Asking questions during a read-aloud provides a chance to connect and talk together in a meaningful way. Children not only fall in love with books and reading but also learn to think deeply, consider other points of view, and listen.

Most good picture books, both fiction and nonfiction, have a story structure. When developing questions to ask children about a book, it is useful to consider these elements:

setting (when and where the story takes place), characters (who the story is about), theme (what the story is about), plot (what happens during the story), and resolution (how the story ends).

A great influence on children's reading motivation and achievement is the opportunity to enjoy high-quality literature. Children who engage in daily discussions about what they read are more likely to become critical readers and learners. Whether reading to one child, a small group, or the whole class, asking in-depth questions based on high-quality children's books promotes discussion and builds literacy skills. Asking questions before, during, and after read-alouds can support language and vocabulary development, comprehension, phonological awareness, and print concepts. Asking higher-level questions helps children understand and make meaning from books.

## Getting Started

Every classroom should have a quiet space that is a defined library or book area. It should have a variety of books conveniently placed for one or more children to look at on their own, along with comfortable seating like a small bench with pillows or some large pillows on the floor. After you read a book to children, place it in the library area so children can revisit the story. Enhance the children's book experiences even more by providing puppets, a feltboard with props from favorite stories, and digital versions of stories.

Reading to a small group of children, or one-to-one, provides a more personal experience and may be preferable when the reason for the read-aloud is very specific. For example, if a child is upset that his mom looks different after undergoing treatment for cancer, you may want to read *Nowhere Hair*, by Sue Glader, illustrated by Edith Buenen, just to him. Or, if a few children have new babies in their families, you might read *Peter's Chair,* by Ezra Jack Keats, to a small group of children.

Often, it is appropriate to read to the entire class. Whether reading with an individual child or doing a read-aloud with the entire group, access to high-quality literature is vital to asking higher-level questions. While individual reading in the library area may be spontaneous, group read-alouds must always be planned. Select books with a topic and vocabulary in mind, and preview them before sharing with children. The first read-aloud of a picture book should always be an uninterrupted reading of the text so children can hear and follow the story as intended. Children need to experience the magic and surprise of the illustrations and the words as each page is turned.

While holding the book so children can see the pictures, begin by reading the title, author, and illustrator, pausing to ask the children to predict from the front cover what they think the book may be about. Any words crucial to understanding the story are also important to share at this time. For example, before reading *Goodnight, Goodnight, Construction Site,* by Sherri Duskey Rinker, illustrated by Tom Lichtenheld, you might say, "What do you think a *construction site* is?," "Have you seen a *construction site*?," and "I wonder why they call it a *construction site*." Children learn new words best when they are presented in

a meaningful context. Providing simple definitions and asking questions that relate to the new words will help expand children's vocabulary and enable them to connect new learning to their prior knowledge and experiences. This technique is also helpful for children who are dual language learners.

## Supporting Children's Learning

Reading the same story over multiple days supports moving from lower- to higher-level thinking. The second read-aloud can be a picture walk where your questions focus on retelling the story through the illustrations or photographs. The pictures complement the text, and the text complements the pictures. Your questions and comments can focus on details from the pictures; for example, "Look at all the hats in the picture. They are all hats, but they are all different. What are some things that are different?" They can also help you add new vocabulary and ask about what is happening in the picture. When reading *I Stink!* by Kate McMullan, illustrated by Jim McMullan, you might say "Does anyone know what a barge is?," "What is the barge doing?," and "What could the garbage truck do if there was no barge?" During third and future reads, you can pause on different pages to ask the class a more complex question, or you can pose varied questions to individual students based on each child's interests and development. However, during a read-aloud, be mindful to limit the time you take to ask questions and make comments. If the story is dragged out too long with interruptions, you lose the children's engagement and may also detract from the story. Some teachers find it helpful to limit the number of questions during the reading to no more than five or six.

After a read-aloud in which you have asked questions beginning at Level 1 (Remember), all the way up to Levels 4 (Analyze) and 5 (Evaluate), don't be afraid to take the experience to the highest level: Level 6 (Create)! Some picture books just beg you to *do* something after the read-aloud. By framing questions and comments that support follow-up in interest areas or with a small group activity, you are naturally guiding your students to tap into high-level thoughts and ideas about how to bring the book to life. Eric Carle's use of watercolors or Lois Ehlert's use of collage, for example, invites children to respond to your questions through artistic expression. Here are some other creations your questions might inspire:

» Making a mural of the characters and setting of book in the art area

» Building the story setting in the block area or recreating the setting in the dramatic play area and dramatizing scenes from the story

» Exploring a concept from a book in the math or science area

» Going outdoors for a walk to observe, explore, or reenact something like what happened in the story

» Making patterns in the math area based on the designs in the book

The key is planning and shaping your questions ahead of time to support these extensions and invite many answers. While Level 1 (Remember) questions are easy to come up with on the spot ("What did the little red hen make?" or "Who did Brown Bear see?"), Level 2 (Understand) questions move beyond simply recalling parts of the story to invite children to talk about the story and the characters. If students don't comprehend the story, they can't move to higher levels of thinking. Level 3 (Apply) questions encourage children to make connections between the story and their own lives or the world around them.

It often takes time to develop and encourage children to answer Level 4 (Analyze) questions, such as "What kinds of things might a dog find to decorate his house in the backyard like the hermit crab decorated his in the ocean?" A graphic organizer like a Venn diagram or two-column chart can be used to facilitate children's responses to Level 4 (Analyze) questions.

Level 5 (Evaluate) questions are appropriate to incorporate during the third or fourth read-aloud of the story and can help children contemplate and solve problems. Lastly, posing Level 6 (Create) questions extends children's thinking about the story even further. These move the read-aloud experience from thinking and comprehending into action.

## The Picture Book Connection

*Chicks and Salsa,* by Aaron Reynolds, illustrated by Paulette Bogan

*Duck! Rabbit!* by Amy Krouse Rosenthal, illustrated by Tom Lichtenheld

*Giraffes Can't Dance,* by Giles Andreae, illustrated by Guy Parker-Rees

*Stand Tall, Molly Lou Melon,* by Patty Lovell, illustrated by David Catrow

*We Found a Hat,* by Jon Klassen

# Expand Children's Thinking and Learning by Asking Questions

**1 Remember**
(identify, name, count, repeat, recall)

- Name one animal that came into the cave while the bear was sleeping. (*Bear Snores On*, by Karma Wilson, illustrated by Jane Chapman)
- Who are the main characters in this story? (*Epossumondas*, by Coleen Salley, illustrated by Janet Stevens)
- What are the two words that rhyme on the first two pages? (*Brown Bear, Brown Bear, What Do You See?* by Bill Martin Jr., illustrated by Eric Carle)

**2 Understand**
(describe, discuss, explain, summarize)

- Tell us about a memory you have. What memory would you give to Miss Nancy? (*Wilfrid Gordon McDonald Partridge*, by Mem Fox, illustrated by Julie Vivas)
- Describe an accessory that you have. (*Fancy Nancy*, by Jane O'Connor, illustrated by Robin Preiss Glasser)
- What happened in the beginning (middle, end) of the story?

**3 Apply**
(explain why, dramatize, identify with/relate to)

- Find some things in this room that are the same shape as one of the shapes in the book. (*Shapes, Shapes, Shapes*, by Tana Hoban)
- What vegetable(s) in this book have you eaten before? (*Rah, Rah, Radishes! A Vegetable Chant*, by April Pulley Sayre)
- How will you use these props to act out what happened in the story?

**4 Analyze**
(recognize change, experiment, infer, compare, contrast)

- Why do you think the author/illustrator made the words look this way on this page? Let me read the line again. (*Don't Let the Pigeon Drive the Bus!* by Mo Willems)
- How was the main character different at the beginning of the story than at the end? Why? (*The Grouchy Ladybug*, by Eric Carle).
- How could you change some of the rhyming words to match the names of other parts of your body you could paint? (*I Ain't Gonna Paint No More!* by Karen Beaumont, illustrated by David Catrow)

**5 Evaluate**
(express opinion, judge, defend/criticize)

- Why do you think Rainbow Fish may have felt that way? (*The Rainbow Fish*, by Marcus Pfister)
- How do you know the dog and bear were friends? (*Dog and Bear: Two Friends, Three Stories*, by Laura Vaccaro Seeger)
- What do you think the peddler learned? (*Caps for Sale: A Tale of a Peddler, Some Monkeys, and Their Monkey Business*, by Esphyr Slobodkina)

**6 Create**
(make, construct, design, author)

- What materials do you need to create the setting for our collage? (*In the Tall, Tall Grass*, by Denise Fleming)
- Make up a song about something you love, like Pete did for his shoes. (*Pete the Cat: I Love My White Shoes*, by Eric Litwin, illustrated by James Dean)
- How would you change the ending?

Of all the gifts with which individuals may be endowed, none emerges earlier than musical talent.

—Howard Gardner, *Frames of Mind: The Theory of Multiple Intelligences*

# Exploring and Making Music

It is mid-October, and in Mr. Schmidt's kindergarten class, the children are singing "The Wheels on the Bus."

After they sing about the door, the horn, the people, and the lights, he comments, "Remember last week when we read the book *The Seals on the Bus* and laughed about all of the silly noises the animals on the bus made? And, when we read *The Wheels on the Tuk Tuk*, we learned some new things to sing about India. The authors of those books made up their own versions of 'The Wheels on the Bus.' Let's compose our own version of the song. What should we sing about?"

The children respond with some new ideas that include the playground, the pizza place, the pumpkin farm, and the bathroom. Mr. Schmidt lists their ideas on the whiteboard and they vote to compose a song about the pizza place.

"Now, how do we have to change the lyrics, or words, of the song to make it fit the tune?"

After a lot of discussion, they come up with three ideas to sing about that have accompanying gestures: "The doughmaker's hands go pound, pound, pound," "The customers in the shop go yum, yum, yum," and "The man at the register goes, 'Here's your change.'" Mr. Schmidt asks the children to sing the song at home that night with their families and to ask family members to add to the verses.

Mr. Schmidt plans to include many more opportunities throughout the year for the children to incorporate their home, family, and school experiences into musical compositions that involve high-level thinking, rhythm, rhyme, and descriptive language.

There are many children's songs that have been adapted into books, including *I Know an Old Teacher*, by Anne Bowen, illustrated by Stephen Gammell ("I Know an Old Lady Who Swallowed a Fly"); *If It's Snowy and You Know It, Clap Your Paws!* by Kim Norman, illustrated by Liza Woodruff ("If You're Happy and You Know It"); and *Over in the Forest: Come and Take a Peek*, by Marianne Berkes, illustrated by Jill Dubin ("Over in the Meadow"), among countless others.

Reading and singing these books as well as comparing and contrasting their characteristics supports high-level thinking. Just asking "Which version do you like better?" does little to encourage children to make deeper connections because it requires only choosing a song or book. However, once you ask "Why?" and other questions, like "What did you notice that was different about the book adaptation from the original song?" and "How can we create our own song to go with the tune?," children engage in deeper learning as they understand, apply, analyze, evaluate, and create.

How young children engage in musical experiences depends on their interests and their individual developmental levels. However, because there are so many ways in which children can connect with music, it is a versatile vehicle for engaging children at any stage in higher-level thinking. When adults provide rich musical experiences infused with thought-provoking questions and comments, children have the opportunity to learn how to identify patterns in rhythms and lyrics in songs, connect emotionally with different types of music, and express themselves verbally and nonverbally—and sometimes with their whole body!

## Getting Started

Use music to help children relax, laugh, pay attention, learn language, and share each other's cultures, home languages, and family heritage. In addition to using classic songs that are often sung in early childhood programs, expose children to developmentally appropriate music from all genres (see "Interesting Music Genres to Explore with Children" below for ideas). When you play a new piece of music for children, ask them to close their

### Interesting Music Genres to Explore with Children

**American folk music:** "Puff, the Magic Dragon," as performed by Peter, Paul, and Mary

**Call and response:** "Did You Feed My Cow?," as performed by Ella Jenkins

**Classical:** "The Carnival of the Animals," composed by Camille Saint-Saëns

**Rap:** "I Saw," as performed by Ella Jenkins

**Reggae:** "One Love," as performed by Bob Marley

**West African chants:** "Toom-Bah-Ee-Lero," as performed by Ella Jenkins

### Quick and Easy Ideas for Making Musical Instruments

**Rhythm sticks:** Tap two sticks or dowels together. To add texture for different sounds, adults can use a striking knife to make notches in the sticks.

**Maracas:** Fill paper towel rolls, yogurt containers, or other reusable materials with beads or similar small items that make pleasant sounds when shaken. Seal with duct tape and decorate.

**Drums:** Cover empty food cans in cloth or vinyl and seal with duct tape or rubber bands. Use wooden spoons, dowels, or pencils with large erasers as drumsticks. Consider including a drum-making kit in your music area, art area, or science area/makerspace. Fill a bin with various materials and encourage children to explore the sounds that they can make with drums they create from the materials. You can do this as a small group activity or with just one or two children in the interest area.

eyes. After the music is finished, ask them what they thought about or imagined while they listened to the music. Encourage them to tell you what the music felt, looked, sounded, and even smelled like. With some practice, this technique can get children to think about music in a deeply imaginative way. To support the home–school connection for children, ask their families to share their favorite music with them. Compare, contrast, revise, and recreate these song lyrics, rhythms, and rhymes as you invite children to participate in higher-level activities inspired by your questions.

## Supporting Children's Learning

There are many melodies that lend themselves to composing new words because they are simple, clear, and easy for children to remember. These include "The Farmer in the Dell," "This Little Light of Mine," "Row, Row, Row Your Boat," and "London Bridge Is Falling Down." Notice that Mr. Schmidt had already exposed his kindergartners to two different versions of "The Wheels on the Bus" before he invited them to create their own rendition of the song. Listening to and singing multiple versions of a song helps children better understand patterns in the melody, rhythm, and lyrics. In this way, they are able to adapt new words to a now-familiar musical framework.

Providing children with opportunities to respond to music with their bodies as well as their voices helps them develop listening skills, vocabulary, and awareness of rhythms, words, and melodies. To expand their musical experiences, have children clap, dance, use scarves, manipulate puppets, and play rhythm instruments. During or after these experiences, ask the children how the music makes them feel or what it makes them think of. Have them think about what it is in the music that evokes those feelings or thoughts; for example, you might ask a child who is listening to a piece of classical music, "How can you imitate the sound of that violin? Does the sound remind you of any other sounds you've heard before?" or "What is it about the deep bass drum that makes you want to stomp your feet like that?"

Music can be integrated at different times throughout the day. For a really wonderful listening experience, try using Sergio Prokofiev's *Peter and the Wolf* during various parts of the daily routine. This symphony for children, written in 1936, is approximately 30 minutes long. Although this seems lengthy for young children, it can provoke some exceptional higher-level conversations about music with older preschoolers and kindergartners.

Introduce it first during nap or rest time, allowing the children to listen to the entire piece while relaxing. Next, play segments of it during whole group time, asking the children to respond to it with their bodies. During small group time or mealtimes, engage the children in discussions about the characters, beginning with some recall and sequencing questions before moving into higher-level inquiries. As the children become more familiar with the piece, ask them what their favorite parts are, how they might change the ending, or what other characters could be part of the story and what the melodies for the new characters might sound like.

## The Picture Book Connection

*I Ain't Gonna Paint No More!* by Karen Beaumont, illustrated by David Catrow

*I See a Song*, by Eric Carle

*Over in the Meadow*, by Olive A. Wadsworth, illustrated by Ezra Jack Keats

*There Was an Old Lady Who Swallowed a Fly*, by Simms Taback

*This Jazz Man*, by Karen Ehrhardt, illustrated by R.G. Roth

# Expand Children's Thinking and Learning by Asking Questions

**1**

**Remember**
(identify, name, count, repeat, recall)

- What were some of the parts of the bus we sang about in "The Wheels on the Bus"?
- What were some of the animals in the song "Big Farm"?
- Tell me the answer to the question "How did you milk her?" in the song "Did You Feed My Cow?"

**2**

**Understand**
(describe, discuss, explain, summarize)

- Which body part did we sing about first (next, last) while singing "La tía Mónica"?
- Tell me what you do with your hands to make that sound on the drum.
- What is this song about? (For a challenge, choose a song in a language other than English that is spoken by one or more of the children. Those children can scaffold the meaning for the others.)

**3**

**Apply**
(explain why, dramatize, identify with/relate to)

- Why do you think Prokofiev used a flute (oboe, clarinet) to portray the bird (duck, cat) in *Peter and the Wolf*?
- How can we act out "Over in the Meadow" while we sing it?
- What other songs have you heard with this instrument in it?

**4**

**Analyze**
(recognize change, experiment, infer, compare, contrast)

- How is "The Wheels on the Bus" the same as (different from) *The Wheels on the Tuk Tuk*?
- What parts of "London Bridge Is Falling Down" changed when we wrote our version, "Ms. William's Class Is Very Smart"?
- What materials could we fill our shakers with to make a musical sound?

**5**

**Evaluate**
(express opinion, judge, defend/criticize)

- Which is your favorite animal (melody) in *Peter and the Wolf*? Why?
- What do you think was the funniest song we created this month? Why?
- Describe the kind of music you think would go with this painting. (Ask the children to do this while you display an image of a famous painting, such as Pollack's *Number 5, 1948* or Monet's *Poplars on the Epte*.)

**6**

**Create**
(make, construct, design, author)

- How will you create a painting (drawing, collage) that shows how you feel when we move to "Toom-Bah-Ee-Lero"?
- What materials should we use to design a mural showing how we feel when we sing "What a Wonderful World"?
- How can we change the words of "Row, Row, Row Your Boat" to sing about our school?

Children of all ages are in love with movement, action, and the self-empowerment that come from learning about, using, and gaining control over their bodies.

—Frances Carlson, *Big Body Play: Why Boisterous, Vigorous, and Very Physical Play Is Essential to Children's Development and Learning*

# Large Motor Activities 10

The kindergartners in Mr. Royce's class are creating a large motor game to use during their unit on ordinal numbers. They develop and test patterns of movement and collectively decide on rules for the game. Mr. Royce incorporates many opportunities for large motor movement into his lesson plans because he has found that his students stay more interested and engaged when they get to move around. He has also noticed that some of his students seem to remember and apply more of what they learn when it is combined with some kind of movement activity. He begins the clapping pattern that signifies the beginning of large motor time—10 claps, alternating fast and slow, because it is ten o'clock in the morning.

Nathaniel and Felipe grab the last of their game materials from the math area and rush over to the carpet.

"We made the rules," Nathaniel exclaims, "and the last rule is that you gotta say the number in English and Spanish!"

Mr. Royce holds up one of the small posters the children created with the number five on it. He asks Felipe to describe to the class the part of the game he and Nathaniel were working on.

Felipe jumps up and explains, "This is our pattern for five. One! Two! Three! Four! Five! Uno! Dos! Tres! Cuatro! Cinco!" Each time he yells a number, he moves his body in a different way. "Okay, ready? Now ask me!"

Nathaniel smiles and says, "What's the fourth thing you did?"

Felipe thinks for a moment and then moves his body into the fourth position of his pattern, bending his knees until he is almost sitting.

"What's the fifth thing?" Nathaniel asks.

Felipe immediately moves his body into his fifth position, arms and legs spread eagle, fingers splayed open, a wide grin on his face.

"Fifth!" Mr. Royce says. "You look like you've really been thinking about this, guys. Felipe, how did you remember which was fifth? That's the highest ordinal number you've done so far!"

Felipe pauses before answering. "I just remember that four was on the floor, and after that was me being giant and giving high fives!"

Mr. Royce listens and nods intently as he explains the connections being made between the high-level math concept and large body movements.

In developmentally appropriate early childhood classrooms, teachers appreciate and encourage children to use their bodies in many different ways, like dancing, moving like different animals, or acting out rain falling down from the sky. Many find that introducing concepts through movement supports not only cognitive learning but also positive behavior. Research shows that the areas of the brain that are activated during academic learning tasks are the same areas a child uses while doing vigorous physical activity, such as jumping up and down or throwing a ball. Moving while learning helps build the connections in a child's brain and solidifies what is being taught along with the movement (Griss 2013).

## Getting Started

A common challenge for many early childhood professionals is offering enough large motor opportunities for children, especially during inclement weather. Combining motor activities with high-level questions supports children's learning *and* their large muscle development and need to move throughout the day. If you are teaching preschoolers and kindergartners about one-to-one correspondence, for example, you might have them stand up at the morning meeting and stomp their feet each time they shout out a number. Ask them, "What are your feet doing each time you shout out a number?" The children are making the connection between the number and the movement.

During whole group meetings, introduce activities such as moving like different animals, parachute games, throwing and catching scarves, and balancing. Along with the motor goals you have for these activities, think about questions you can correlate to their movements to encourage the children to experience the activity in a deeper way.

During balancing activities, for example, the main goal might be to build large motor strength and coordination. Core strength and balance are precursors for many tasks, from hopping, skipping, and jumping to holding a pencil. As you challenge children to keep their bodies balanced while moving in different ways, encourage them to compare the feelings the movements are creating and how different muscles are engaged in different positions. For example, after introducing the vocabulary word *balance* and directing them to assume a specific position, ask, "What body part you are balancing on?" and "How does your body feel while you're balancing on one foot?" Challenge the children to identify the other parts of their body they're using to balance on one foot. This will help them become more aware of what the rest of their body is doing in order to keep them upright. To extend this activity, provide items for them to balance on different parts of their bodies, such as beanbags, small manipulatives, or scarves. Offer wooden unit blocks of various sizes for the children to stand on to compare how the size of the block affects their balance.

## Supporting Children's Movement and Learning

To give children as many opportunities as possible for large motor activity, consider ways to design an indoor playground. Using portable equipment and stationary furniture, work with the children to create obstacle courses or stations in the classroom. Here are some suggestions.

» **Swatting balloons with foam noodles:** Hang balloons from the ceiling or wall at varying heights and encourage the children to swat at them using foam noodles. Ask questions like, "What happens to the balloon when you hit it really hard?," "What happens when you hit it softly?," and "Which balloon was the easiest (most difficult) for you to hit and why?"

- *Safety note:* Limit this activity to two or three children at a time to avoid conflict or inappropriate use of materials.

» **"Skating and skiing":** Give each child two paper plates or cardboard squares to place under their feet to "skate" across the carpet. Alternatively, children can use carpet squares to "ski" across linoleum or tile floors (Torbert & Schneider 1993). Ask questions like "What happens when you lift your feet off the paper plates (cardboard squares, carpet squares)?" and "What is another way to skate using your feet, hands, knees, or another body part?"

- *Safety note:* Challenge children to pass one another without touching. This offers an additional level of difficulty while encouraging children to maintain personal space and minimize crashing.

» **Hollow block balance beam:** Line up long wooden blocks to create a balance beam and encourage children to walk across it. Make this more challenging by creating a stepping pattern on the balance beam. Ask questions like "What happens to your balance when you put your arms above your head instead of out to the side?"

- *Safety note:* For younger children, arrange the balance beam near something sturdy they can hold to assist with balance. Make sure there are no sharp corners in the vicinity that children could potentially fall onto.

» **Spiderwebs:** Weave crepe paper streamers in and out of the furniture at varying heights for children to navigate through. This activity encourages planning, coordination, and spatial awareness. Ask questions like "What's your plan for going through those next two rows of spiderwebs?," "Will you go under or over?," and "Which area was the most difficult (easiest) to pass through and why?"

- *Safety note:* Crepe paper streamers allow the children to make mistakes without getting hurt. If a child trips on one of the webs or gets stuck, the paper will simply break. To offer older children a greater challenge, use yarn or string. These will not break if a child gets caught up, so limit this activity to two or three children at a time and increase supervision.

As children become more in tune with the movements of their body and the vocabulary associated with it, continue to ask questions and make comments to extend their learning. Incorporate big body play into your daily routine, and keep your students moving and learning!

### The Picture Book Connection

*Clap Your Hands,* by Lorinda Bryan Cauley

*Dance!* by Bill T. Jones

*From Head to Toe,* by Eric Carle

*Hop, Hop, Jump!* by Lauren Thompson, illustrated by Jarrett J. Krosoczka

*The Squiggle,* by Carole Lexa Schaefer, illustrated by Pierr Morgan

# Expand Children's Thinking and Learning by Asking Questions

### 1   **Remember**
(identify, name, count, repeat, recall)

- What is that movement you are doing with your hands called?
- How many times did you stomp your feet?
- What are you balancing on your head?

### 2   **Understand**
(describe, discuss, explain, summarize)

- Which part of your body did you touch first (second, third)?
- How do your arms and legs move when you pretend to climb a tree?
- How did you keep the beanbag on your head while you marched to the music?

### 3   **Apply**
(explain why, dramatize, identify with/relate to)

- What other letters could you make using your arms and legs?
- Why do you think your knees bend right before you jump?
- You're rolling fast across the carpet! What else rolls?

### 4   **Analyze**
(recognize change, experiment, infer, compare, contrast)

- Which is easier to balance on your head, the toy car or the baby doll? Why?
- How does the scarf change when we wave it in different ways to the different rhythms?
- I wonder what would happen if you tried jumping up and down while bouncing the ball at the same time.

### 5   **Evaluate**
(express opinion, judge, defend/criticize)

- Do you think your baby sister would be able to balance on one foot like you are? Why or why not?
- Which activity did you like better—when we used our bodies to act out *We're Going on a Bear Hunt* or *We're Going on a Lion Hunt*? Why?
- How should we change the obstacle course so that we can eliminate the problems we are having with it now?

### 6   **Create**
(make, construct, design, author)

- Create a pattern using different kinds of jumps.
- Choreograph a dance that shows how a flower changes as it blooms.
- Make up a game that uses jumping, hoops, and counting.

Because the teachers and children's minds meet on matters of real interest to both, teachers' minds are also engaged. They seem intent on listening closely to the children's suggestions and questions, probing their thinking, making suggestions, and encouraging children to respond to each others' ideas.

—Carolyn Edwards, Lella Gandini, and George Forman, *The Hundred Languages of Children: The Reggio Emilia Approach—Advanced Reflections,* Second Edition

# Outdoors

Sue Mankiw

Red, yellow, and brown leaves are crunching underfoot as the children from the family center's preschool class hold the rings of the walking rope tightly and tromp along the winding pathways at Central Park. This outdoor adventure is part of their weekly routine. Mr. Joe and his assistant teacher, Ms. Aida, empty backpacks filled with clipboards, brown paper bags, and digital cameras. The children select their tools and scramble off to visit Todd, the big oak tree the class adopted on the first day of school.

Within minutes, one of the students, Jayden, exclaims, "Look! Nuts are falling from Todd's branches!"

"Those aren't nuts, they're acorns. Right, Mr. Joe?" asks Elijah.

As the two boys begin putting the acorns in their paper bags, Jayden says, "Look, that squirrel likes the nuts, too."

Mr. Joe writes down their exact words and takes photos of their discoveries. He is reminded of the storybook, *Nuts to You!* by Lois Ehlert, and he jots down some high-level questions to ask the children later: *What did you notice today when you visited Todd?*, *What did you discover that was different than last week?*, *Are acorns a kind of nut?*, and *Why do you think squirrels like nuts?* Mr. Joe looks forward to hearing the children's responses when they revisit their trip to the park during small group time.

Outdoor spaces provide a wealth of topics for children and teachers to explore. Mr. Joe has set the stage for ongoing learning opportunities by creating a weekly routine that focuses on the children's in-depth study of Todd, the adopted oak tree. The park is just one example of an outdoor space where children can develop and apply new knowledge. To develop critical thinking skills, children must build background knowledge from multiple sources and experiences.

## Getting Started

The development of critical thinking skills depends heavily upon background knowledge and language development, which increase when children have frequent opportunities to interact in a developmentally appropriate manner with the environment, materials, adults,

## Outdoor Spaces and Experiences

Consider some of the following outdoor spaces for exploration:

- Playground
- Garden
- Outside the window
- Park
- Zoo
- Neighborhood
- Beach
- Porch or deck
- Backyard

Ideally, children can play uninterrupted and roam about in safe, interesting outdoor spaces for extended periods of time. Because not every early childhood environment offers all of these advantages, teachers find ways to bring a variety of outdoor experiences into the classroom, such as

- Hanging a bird feeder in the classroom window
- Placing a weather watch station at one window
- Sitting outside on the porch or deck
- Putting snow in the sand and water table (alternately, in pots or buckets) in the winter
- Setting up a science area with tools to investigate pumpkins

Even when you can offer multiple outdoor experiences, it is a good idea to extend experiences back into the classroom.

and each other. Therefore, much depends on the intentionality of the teacher. Mr. Joe is intentional in his actions and has based his decisions on several principles.

**Set the stage for learning.** Mr. Joe knows that children are more likely to ask and answer higher-level questions when exciting things are happening in their world. Make a commitment to locate new, interesting outdoor spaces in your community that children can explore over an extended period of time and that inspire children's curiosity, which will stimulate their own questions and encourage them to investigate further. Consider children's physical and developmental needs, and choose locations that are inclusive and accessible to all children. Take the lead from the children. Allow children to be active participants in their own learning and to make their own choices. When you take a neighborhood walk, listen carefully to the things that the children notice and are curious about. Or, ask questions about the things that children see from the windows of your classroom to learn about what is interesting to them.

**Provide tools for outdoor exploration.** When children have access to scientific tools (clipboards, cameras, specimen bags, magnifying glasses, binoculars), they are more likely to take on the role of explorers and scientists. Tools empower children to become serious in their study and explorations; they give children a method to gather and record information, and they promote an inquiry-based curriculum, which leads to more in-depth questions.

**Remember that children's interactions with each other are as important as their interactions with adults.** Give children opportunities to have conversations without adult

interruption. Listen carefully to children's talk. Record and document their learning (what they say and do). Don't expect that they will remember everything that happened earlier in the day or the day before. Use photographs and real-life objects from their explorations, such as the brown bags filled with acorns, to help them revisit and reconnect to prior learning experiences. Write down their questions as they come up in conversation.

**Make learning visible.** Create documentation boards with photographs and children's words, including their observations and questions. Put these at the children's eye level and display them for an extended period of time before rotating them out to feature other works. This allows you and the children to revisit their learning. Then, as they mature and develop critical thinking skills, they can continue conversations about topics in which they are interested.

**Make connections to children's literature as well as print and online informational resources to help children find answers to their questions.** Although some informational resources may appear to have too much text for young children, the photos and realistic illustrations intrigue them and often lead to richer conversations and further inquiry. You can also invite experts to come in as a resource. Support children in developing their own open-ended questions for the individual ahead of time. Be prepared to include and support dual language learners and families. In your conversations and during read-alouds, do your best to translate key words related to outdoor content and concepts into children's home languages. To strengthen your partnership with families, use their home languages in your communications with them, such as emails, newsletters, storybooks sent home, and documentation boards. Technology can be a powerful tool here. Not only can the Internet provide a wealth of visual resources that help transcend language barriers—

such as video clips, animations, and photos—it is also a resource for translating words and simple phrases. Guide children in their search for an informational video clip or image by helping them identify letters while typing a search word on the keyboard.

## Supporting Children's Play and Learning

Back in the classroom after visiting Todd at the park, Mr. Joe looks at his notes. He evaluates the levels of his questions based on what the children had to say during their excursion. He decides he will read the children the storybook he was reminded of earlier, *Nuts to You!,* and he writes a few more questions to accompany the story. Later in the day, Mr. Joe gathers a small group of children to talk about their trip to see Todd.

To help the children evaluate and problem solve the question of whether an acorn is a nut, Mr. Joe has selected and placed some materials on a table in the science area: acorns and walnuts, a few with their shells cracked open; scientific tools, like magnifying glasses and rulers; and a few copies of an informational book titled *Tell Me, Tree: All About Trees for Kids,* by Gail Gibbons. The question of the day is written on the whiteboard: *Is an acorn a nut? Why or why not?* Later, he will join the children as they explore and discuss the characteristics of the walnuts and the acorns, look through the books, and place a sticky note with their name and their answer for the question of the day on the whiteboard.

Mr. Joe understands that before children can create, they must have a strong foundation of background knowledge. He has set the stage for the class to make, construct, design, or author something new based on what they know. He includes blank notebooks and picture cards with words (*Todd, oak tree, nut, acorn, walnut, squirrel, leaf*) in the writing area. Mr. Joe also adds loose parts, such as branches and acorns, to the block, dramatic play, and art areas. As he observes dramatizations and constructions based on the children's newfound outdoor knowledge, Mr. Joe will continue to listen carefully and document the children's actions and use of new vocabulary as they discuss and explain their creations.

Outdoor spaces open the door to a wide, rich variety of inquiry and natural opportunities for critical thinking. Mr. Joe is pleased with his progress as an intentional teacher. He is becoming more skilled each day in planning higher-level questions and creating them on the spot. His documentation of the children's language and actions is more detailed and purposeful. To help him hone his skills, he has begun to periodically document and reflect upon all of his questions as well as the children's questions. He will use this documentation as a guide for future lessons.

### The Picture Book Connection

*Everybody Needs a Rock,* by Byrd Baylor, illustrated by Peter Parnall

*The Green Line,* by Polly Farquharson

*Hello Ocean/Hola Mar,* by Pam Muñoz Ryan, illustrated by Mark Astrella

*My Steps,* by Sally Derby, illustrated by Adjoa J. Burrowes

*Outside Your Window: A First Book of Nature,* by Nicola Davies, illustrated by Mark Hearld

*Peterson Field Guides for Young Naturalists* are also wonderful resources for the science and/or library areas.

# Expand Children's Thinking and Learning by Asking Questions

| | | |
|---|---|---|
| 1 | **Remember**<br>(identify, name, count, repeat, recall) | • What kind of tree is Todd?<br>• What animals did we see in the park?<br>• How many swings do we have on our playground? |
| 2 | **Understand**<br>(describe, discuss, explain, summarize) | • What did you notice today when we visited the car wash?<br>• Why is it important to put birdseed in the feeders every day during the winter?<br>• What are some other things we can do when we play outside? |
| 3 | **Apply**<br>(explain why, dramatize, identify with/relate to) | • What can you do with your body to make yourself look just like Todd, the oak tree?<br>• Why do you think the squirrels liked the acorns?<br>• Where have you seen this kind of fence before? Why do you think people need fences? |
| 4 | **Analyze**<br>(recognize change, experiment, infer, compare, contrast) | • Let's take a look at a picture of our visit to Todd last week and a picture from this morning. What is different about Todd than the last time we visited?<br>• Some of you are saying we found acorns and some are saying they are nuts. I wonder how we can figure out whether they are acorns or nuts.<br>• Look, there is a store here right next to a house. What is the same (different) about the storefront and the house? |
| 5 | **Evaluate**<br>(express opinion, judge, defend/criticize) | • Today we learned about hermit crabs and how they protect themselves by living in shells. I wonder if any other animals use a shell to protect themselves. What do you think?<br>• Which do you think is the oldest (strongest, most beautiful) tree? Why?<br>• If there could be only one type of plant on the street where you live, what plant would you choose? Why? |
| 6 | **Create**<br>(make, construct, design, author) | • I've added *Nuts to You!* by Lois Ehlert to the block area, along with some tree blocks, plastic squirrels, leaves, and acorns. What kinds of constructions will you create with these materials this week?<br>• What will you add to our mural to remind us of all of the things we saw on our walk?<br>• What will you add to our class book, *What We Know About Trees*? |

Today is Monday
Monday—string beans
All you hungry children, come and eat it up!

—Traditional children's folk song

# Mealtimes

Kristie Redner

**12**

It is one of the most anticipated times of the day in Ms. Coletta's 3-year-old preschool classroom . . . lunch! Some children bring in something to eat from home (juice or water, a snack, or even a full meal), while the others wait their turn to serve themselves the school lunch. Conversation flows around the tables.

Ms. Coletta notices that Mika has taken out some dumplings and chopsticks from her lunchbox and says, "That looks delicious! What is that called?"

"Dumplings," replies Mika.

Another child asks her, "Why do you use sticks? Where's your fork?"

"They're chopsticks. I can push my food onto them to eat," Mika answers, demonstrating. "Like this."

Ms. Coletta adds, "It's another way to put your food in your mouth. Remember the book we read together earlier in the week called *Spoon?* We can read it again later and talk about what kinds of food we can eat with different utensils. We also have some chopsticks in the dramatic play area that you can try to use to pick up some pretend food after naptime."

Meanwhile, at the other table, Danika peeks at the empanada Lisette brought from home. "Oh, I like that! My mommy, she gives me that at home. It's so good!"

Lisette replies, "It's my favorite, favorite, favorite."

The teacher assistant, Naomi, pretends to take a bite and says, "Scrumptious! I love to eat empanadas, too. My favorite is with chicken and hot sauce. What kind do you like?"

The other children at the table join in the conversation, with each child proclaiming his or her favorite food. Naomi encourages the children to talk to each other about the foods they love and, noticing the enthusiasm of the empanada discussion, she uses the opportunity to extend the learning by asking the children how they think empanadas are made. She makes note of what they say to share it with Ms. Coletta after lunch. Maybe she could incorporate it in a lesson.

Mealtimes, especially for hungry young children, are an exciting, busy time of the day. There is much anticipation about eating lunch after a busy morning of working, creating, and thinking. It can also be a relaxing time, a part of the daily routine that naturally leads to conversations and questions about food, likes and dislikes, self-help skills ("I can't open my milk. Can you help me?"), and a host of other topics important to the children. This part of the daily routine is an excellent time to extend children's thinking by asking a variety of questions or sharing your observations.

## Getting Started

Mealtimes naturally lend themselves to sharing family customs and traditions involving food. They are also times when children begin to independently solve simple problems (clean up spills, figure out how many napkins to distribute) and help each other. By asking questions that prompt children to think of ideas and solutions and supporting their growing abilities to do things themselves, you can promote children's social and emotional development and their self-sufficiency.

Three-, 4-, and 5-year-old children take pride in performing tasks for themselves. The entire mealtime routine—washing hands, opening food containers, serving themselves a school lunch, throwing away trash—is geared toward fostering independence. Even eating with utensils instead of with their hands is a big accomplishment for young children. Talking about *why* people usually use utensils to eat can open up a conversation that most

students can join. Expanding on that conversation by talking about some foods that we *do* eat with our hands and comparing them to those we usually eat with utensils expands children's understanding. By asking high-level questions that help children think deeper than simple yes-or-no answers, you can encourage them to broaden the scope of their language and cognition. For example, "Why do you think we eat at the table rather than on our cots?" requires more thought and more complex vocabulary than "What do you like to eat?"

Once you start to use mealtimes as springboards for in-depth conversations with students, you will see the excitement on their faces as they talk about food experiences, preferences, and traditions and help each other serve, clean up, and enjoy eating together. This is a great chance for you to share your own preferences, traditions, and cooking and eating habits with the children, too. Mealtimes are a time when other topics are often discussed—a family vacation, a new pet, or a popular movie several of the children have seen. You can use the same questioning techniques discussed here to support these topics of discussion. Children will be eager to engage in high-level thinking and learning about a topic they themselves have chosen.

## Supporting Children's Language Learning

Children's language development, especially in a multilingual classroom, varies a great deal. Some children converse fluently in one or two languages, while others observe, are nonverbal, or speak only in their home language. Because of this wide disparity in language skills, asking higher-level questions can be a challenge. However, there are some strategies you can use to include all children in discussions. Mealtimes offer a wonderful gateway for conversations, since talking about food is a concrete topic that all children can relate to.

Asking families to help translate some key questions, such as those presented in the opening scenario, can create a bridge of communication between school and home (see "Questions to Ask During Mealtimes" on page 146). Encouraging families to ask the same questions at home and share with you their children's responses helps children to take part in their families' experiences, gives them a common topic to talk about, and supports language development.

### The Picture Book Connection

*Bread, Bread, Bread*, by Ann Morris, photographs by Ken Heyman

*Green Eggs and Ham*, by Dr. Seuss

*Rah, Rah, Radishes! A Vegetable Chant*, by April Pulley Sayre

*Spoon*, by Amy Krouse Rosenthal, illustrated by Scott Magoon

*Yummy! Good Food Makes Me Strong!* by Shelley Rotner and Sheila M. Kelly

# Expand Children's Thinking and Learning by Asking Questions

**1 Remember**
(identify, name, count, repeat, recall)

- What did you have for breakfast?
- What snacks does your family eat?
- What shapes are the foods on your plate?

**2 Understand**
(describe, discuss, explain, summarize)

- I see your sandwich today has a lot of ingredients! Describe some of them for us.
- Tell us about where you eat most of your meals. Who usually eats with you?
- Explain how the adults in your family cook your meals. What ingredients do they put in the foods? How do they cook the meals?

**3 Apply**
(explain why, dramatize, identify with/relate to)

- Which pictures in *Bread, Bread, Bread* remind you of your home and family? Why?
- Show us how you sit and eat at home. What kinds of things do you talk about or do while you eat at home?
- Pretend you invited a friend to eat dinner at your house. How would you cook and serve the food? What would your family serve?

**4 Analyze**
(recognize change, experiment, infer, compare, contrast)

- Yesterday at small group time, we drew pictures of our favorite foods. How is your picture the same as (different from) the pictures your friends drew?
- This morning we read *Rah, Rah, Radishes! A Vegetable Chant* and *Go, Go, Grapes! A Fruit Chant*. What did you notice about them that is the same (different)?
- What happens when you sit with your chair far away from the table and your feet up compared to when you sit with your tummy pressed close to the table and your feet on the floor?

**5 Evaluate**
(express opinion, judge, defend/criticize)

- Is your favorite meal nutritious for you? Why or why not?
- What could we do to make our meals healthier (e.g., drink water instead of soda)?
- How do you think your friend feels when you touch his food and kick him under the table? Where might be a better place to put your hands and feet so he doesn't feel bothered?

**6 Create**
(make, construct, design, author)

- I wonder how you could create this lunch by using playdough or some of the recycled materials in the art area. Maybe after lunch you could try out some of your ideas.
- Pretend you are eating your favorite meal, and all of a sudden, an alien comes down from a spaceship and says, "I've never seen any of this food before. Tell me about it!" What would you say? Let's make a story out of it.
- How can we make a list for the dramatic play area showing some of the foods we eat at home and at school? Where can we find photos of all those foods? How do we make it into a menu with words and pictures?

# More Learning
# Opportunities
# with Questions

Life for young children is shaped by relationships. Wherever they spend their time, they need to be cared for by adults who are able to invest emotionally in their well-being—adults who care *about* them, not just *for* them.

—Amy C. Baker and Lynn A. Manfredi/Petitt, *Relationships, the Heart of Quality Care: Creating Community Among Adults in Early Care Settings*

# Supporting Emotional Development During the First Months of School

Kristie Redner

It is arrival time, and children are coming into the mixed-age preschool classroom to begin their day. Ana was absent the day before, and the teacher, Mrs. Corbacho, says, "Oh, Ana, welcome back. I missed you yesterday!"

Darnell, another child, repeats the greeting to Ana, and comes over to give her a hug. Ana sniffs, bursts into tears, and cries, "I want my mommy!"

Several children come over to see what the commotion is about. Mrs. Corbacho sits down and holds Ana on her lap. "You seem upset, Ana. Do you want help from a few friends to make you feel better?"

Ana nods her head, so Mrs. Corbacho tells the children gathered around, "Ana is feeling sad today. Does anyone have an idea why she's so sad?"

The children discuss some reasons why Ana could be crying—maybe she wants her mom/dad/grandma, she forgot a toy at home she wants to play with, or she has a tummy ache.

Mrs. Corbacho says, "I think Ana is feeling so sad because she misses her mommy. Sometimes, I miss my mommy too, and I feel sad. Sometimes it's hard, isn't it?" Ana nods her head and puts her hands around the teacher's neck. Mrs. Corbacho asks the other children, "How can we help our friend Ana feel better?"

One child runs to give Ana a tissue to dry her eyes. Another gives her the aromatherapy pillow from her cubby.

"Let's go to the zen garden!" exclaims Darnell.

Someone gets the class yoga book and shows Ana the photograph of her doing her favorite pose.

Mrs. Corbacho then comments, "I wonder if anyone can create a picture for Ana. Maybe you can draw a time when you felt sad, and then draw what you did to make yourself feel better." As Ana calms down, the teacher gives her a hug. "Look how much your friends love you. They gave you tissues, brought you your aromatherapy pillow, and are even drawing pictures for you. They all care about you so much!"

Ana nods, starting to smile, then goes to hang up her backpack in her cubby. She is ready to start the day.

Especially during the first month of school, young children experience a tidal wave of emotions—fear, anger, sadness, excitement, and joy. Many are leaving their family for an extended amount of time for the first time, and some may experience anxiety when the adult who has likely been their primary caregiver since birth leaves them with someone else (Berk 2003). The intensity of emotions can be overwhelming for children and teachers alike, so having some practical ways of helping children cope with their feelings and express them in appropriate ways—as depicted in the opening vignette—is essential to maintaining a peaceful, well-balanced classroom. You can use a variety of techniques and higher-level questioning strategies to help children examine their emotions in a safe environment.

As children take on new challenges at school—for example, how to zip their jacket, open a milk carton, or finally build a tower that doesn't fall down immediately—they experience a range of emotions as they try, learn, and eventually succeed. All emotions that children experience can be discussed and better understood using higher-level questioning. For example, asking children to draw a picture that shows a time when they were feeling happy and encouraging them to talk about what they were doing that made them feel that way is one avenue for children to concretely examine and identify their emotions.

## Getting Started

To set a tone of inclusive acceptance for all children in the classroom and provide an atmosphere of emotional security, the first step is to show children that you genuinely care for them. Children need to feel secure, to feel that the people who care for them acknowledge and support their feelings. Recognizing and labeling how they feel help young learners feel in control of their emotions. For example, in the opening vignette Mrs. Corbacho mentions that Ana was missed when she was absent. Letting a child know that you are glad to have her in the group helps form the very basis of emotional development: love and acceptance.

Another benefit of helping children identify and gain control of their emotions is that they will feel that they are a part of an authentic classroom community where they know they are comfortable and cared for. When teachers model kindness, attentiveness, and genuine enjoyment in being a part of the classroom, children learn these important social skills through what they observe. By asking children questions about their emotions, you draw attention to their feelings and emotions and provide the opportunity for children to examine them closer.

## Supporting Children's Emotional Development

As children grow more independent, their self-confidence builds. As the year goes on, ask children to think of everyday activities (or you can start by pointing them out yourself) they can do now at school that they couldn't when they were younger. Make a classroom book entitled *I'm Proud Because I Can Do It!* and include photographs of children doing these activities, such as writing their names, constructing a tower, using a computer, scaling a climber outside, or sorting rocks. Ask children to describe how they learned a particular skill or achieved a milestone and to think about how they might help someone else learn that skill. Keep the book in your classroom library area and refer to it throughout the year. Children will gravitate toward this tangible evidence of their growth and feel proud of their achievements.

Alternative techniques can also be used to give children ways to handle their strong emotions, including aromatherapy pillows, yoga, and a zen garden. An aromatherapy pillow is a small cloth bag or pillow that contains an herbal teabag. Children can choose their favored tea scent, put it in their pillow, and store it in their cubby. When they are feeling overwhelmed by negative emotions, encourage them to cuddle their pillow and inhale its scent. By taking deep breaths and slowing down their breathing, they will self-soothe.

Stretching and moving their bodies is another way children can release strong emotions. Set up a small yoga mat and related books in a quiet area in the classroom. *Little Yoga: A Toddler's First Book of Yoga* is an excellent resource to teach children poses, which are compared to different animal movements (for example, Tree Pose is likened to a wobbling "little bird"). You might also create a unique class yoga book by photographing the children in their favorite poses and assembling the photos in a book or a display.

A zen garden is another effective method of calming down. To make one, you need a tray of sand, a small rake (a back scratcher or a fork can be used), and some rocks. Teach children to use the rake to slowly move the rocks and make designs in the sand. This activity is meant for only one child at a time, and it should be set up on a table in a quiet corner of the classroom. The intentionally slow, small movements of this activity help calm the mind and give the child a focused way to regain control of his emotions.

## The Picture Book Connection

*Little Yoga: A Toddler's First Book of Yoga*, by Rebecca Whitford, illustrated by Martina Selway

*Owl Babies*, by Martin Waddell, illustrated by Patrick Benson

*The Peace Book*, by Todd Parr

*The Story of Ferdinand*, by Munro Leaf, illustrated by Robert Lawson

*When Sophie Gets Angry—Really, Really Angry . . .* by Molly Bang

# Expand Children's Thinking and Learning by Asking Questions

## 1 Remember
(identify, name, count, repeat, recall)

- What is it called when we do movement poses to keep our bodies and minds feeling good?
- How many deep breaths will you take to relax? Let's count.
- What shape are you making with your rake in the zen garden sand?

## 2 Understand
(describe, discuss, explain, summarize)

- How does this part of the story make you feel? (Refer to the children's books at the end of this chapter.)
- What is something you can do if you feel sad, angry, or upset to make yourself (or a friend) feel better?
- What happened first that made you upset today in the dramatic play area? What happened next? How were you feeling then?

## 3 Apply
(explain why, dramatize, identify with/relate to)

- Using puppets, present a scenario where a child is feeling cared for and loved (e.g., when a caregiver leaves and the teacher holds the child's hand). Ask the student to act out what the puppet can do to support that positive emotion.
- Tell me about a time when you felt proud because you were able to do something new.
- Can you think of a time when you felt glad and peaceful inside? Where were you? Who were you with?

## 4 Analyze
(recognize change, experiment, infer, compare, contrast)

- Show me an angry (sad, upset) face. Tell me about a time when you were angry. Now show me an excited face. Tell me about a time when you were excited. Which emotion do you like feeling? Why? How does your body feel when you are angry? When you are excited?
- If a friend shares the LEGO bricks with you when you sit down next to him, how does it make you feel? Do you feel different when someone doesn't want to play LEGO bricks with you?
- Using a book such as *When Sophie Gets Angry—Really, Really Angry . . .* by Molly Bang, show the illustrations and ask students to describe Sophie's two extreme emotions: anger and being calm.

## 5 Evaluate
(express opinion, judge, defend/criticize)

- Why do you think children sometimes feel sad (angry, upset) when they come to school (leave their family)?
- If you see your friend fall down on the playground, what do you think you could do to help her feel safe and loved?
- When you're so upset that you feel like yelling or throwing something, why is it a good idea to calm yourself using yoga, playing in the zen garden, or smelling your aromatherapy pillow?

## 6 Create
(make, construct, design, author)

- Draw a picture of how you felt when you were sad (angry, upset) before you smelled your aromatherapy pillow (did yoga, played in the zen garden, blew some bubbles) and then draw a picture of how you felt after. Are they the same? Why or why not?
- How can we design an area in our classroom for a friend to go to if she is feeling sad and wants to be alone? What kinds of materials should we put in this area?
- Which yoga pose would you like me to photograph you in for your page in our classroom yoga book?

Change is the law of life. And those who look only to the past or the present are certain to miss the future.

—John F. Kennedy, address at St. Paul's Church in Frankfurt, Germany, on June 25, 1963

# Kickstarting the School Year: Exploring Change Through Long-Term Studies

**14**

After taking several walks around the school grounds in September, Mr. Jacobs's new class of 3-year-olds decides that the grassy spot underneath the large maple tree is their favorite place for snack time.

Moustafa looks up, pointing at the canopy of leaves. "Green!"

His teacher smiles and says, "Yes, all the leaves are green. Soon it will be autumn, and they will all turn red."

Moustafa looks at the tree and then back at his teacher, asking, "Red?"

Mr. Jacobs decides to help the children expand their vocabulary and learn about the seasons by having them observe how the maple tree changes over the school year. He takes a photo of the tree and later prints it out. Several children gather around as he labels the photo *Observation 1: September* and displays it on the far left edge of the long bulletin board that hangs at the children's eye level. This begins the change line the children will add to for the rest of the year.

"What are some things you notice in this photo?" Mr. Jacobs asks the children. He recognizes that many of them have limited vocabulary and are new to school, so he begins with a lower-level question to begin building vocabulary and conversation skills. Mr. Jacobs knows that over time, this project will give the class opportunities to learn descriptive words about the color, size, and shape of the tree. In addition, many children will notice, compare, and contrast the changes in the sky, grass, and animals throughout the year.

Victoria, a verbal 3½-year-old, points to the photo. "I got a tree at my house and it's got five leaves on the ground but yellow."

Her teacher immediately picks up on the teachable moment to scaffold her knowledge with a higher-level question. "Victoria, what looks different about this tree than the one at your house with five yellow leaves on the ground?"

Victoria and her teacher begin a thoughtful exchange about what might start to happen to the maple tree as the school year progresses.

Did you ever have a great idea near the end of a school year and think to yourself, "I wish I had started this back in September"? The beginning of the school year is the perfect time to begin a long-term study in your classroom. Projects that focus on tracking changes over a long period of time give children the opportunity to *observe* changes that take place in nature, people, and the built environment; *document* what they observe; *reflect* on why change occurs; and *predict* future changes. Think of such projects as scientific longitudinal studies!

Mr. Jacobs might use these same terms when speaking to his class about the maple tree study throughout the year:

» "We are going to look at this tree and talk about what we see. We're going to *observe* it."

» "Let's write down (draw, take pictures of) what the tree looks like right now. We are going to *document* our observations so that we don't forget what we saw today. What are some other ways we can *document* what we notice?"

» "Let's think about what we have seen over the past few months and how the tree has been changing. We're going to *reflect* on what we've done. How has the tree changed since last week? since September?"

» "The tree has changed so much! Can you guess what it might look like the next time we visit? Let's *predict* what changes will happen."

## Getting Started

Do you have a stream close to your school? Is there a new shopping mall under construction within walking distance? Are plans underway to add outdoor music, new large motor activities, or a vegetable garden to your playground? These topics and many others lend themselves to long-term studies. They offer multiple opportunities for children to observe, document, reflect, and predict. Consider many ideas—keep yourself informed about your school, the community, the natural environment, and the unique experiences and situations that the children and their families are excited about.

You may find that new ideas for long-term studies emerge from the children during thoughtful discussions about change. You can ask questions like "What are your favorite things that you see while walking to school?" and "I brought in a few photos of some really neat art called *installation art*. It's like the junk building we do in the art area but really big, and it's outside! The artist transforms a huge space with a three-dimensional work they create, add to, and change over time. What do you see in these photos?" You can use descriptions and questions like these to initiate conversations during group times or while casually chatting at the lunch table.

Some topics for long-term studies that work wonderfully with young children include

» Creating an indoor or outdoor art installation

» Studying the development of a child's infant sibling or young pet

» Watching a construction project, such as a building or new landscaping

» Observing a natural object, like a tree or plot of land

As you consider what to focus on for a long-term study, ask yourself whether the subject

» Interests the children

» Provides consistent opportunities for observation

» Allows the children to see noticeable changes over time

## Supporting Children's Learning

You can choose whether to go more in depth with an investigation or use a long-term study as an interesting, practical way to incorporate high-level interactions into your curriculum even when you have other day-to-day activities going on. The children can be focused on it for days at a time, or it can simply exist in the background.

With the children, you can create a timeline, or "change line," that shows the changes in what you are studying together. This visual representation, like a timeline, starts with what the children observe today and moves to the right in a linear way. The change line becomes a permanent interactive display in the classroom, just like the daily routine chart or class helper chart. Children can use the change line to reflect on their own or during more formal learning activities you plan. Engage children in this display by starting with simple questions such as "How many photos have we taken so far?" and "Tell me about what you see in this first photo. How about in the second photo?" Then move on to higher-level questions like "How does this tree limb look different in these two photos? What changed?" or "What might happen to our photos if we stand under the tree to take the picture instead of in front of it?"

One of the following change line ideas could be a great choice for organizing and displaying the documentation of your long-term study:

» Create and add to a horizontal change line placed at children's eye level on the wall.

» Create and add to a vertical change line starting from the floor and moving upward.

» Collect children's writing, photos, and drawings in a large book or binder over the course of the project.

» Tape photos to unit blocks so children can build and sequence with them in the block area.

» String up a clothesline in your classroom and hang up the children's writing, photos, and drawings with clothespins. This could also be used as a self-correcting, sequencing game. Number the documentation items, mix them up, and have the children place them in the correct order based on what is shown or described.

The table on page 97 features some ideas for implementing long-term studies, along with tips to help you get organized.

## The Picture Book Connection

*Do You Know Which Ones Will Grow?* by Susan A. Shea, illustrated by Tom Slaughter

*How a House Is Built,* by Gail Gibbons

*A Leaf Can Be . . .* by Laura Purdie Salas, illustrated by Violeta Dabija

*Road Builders,* by B.G. Hennessy, illustrated by Simms Taback

*When I Was Little: A Four-Year-Old's Memoir of Her Youth,* by Jamie Lee Curtis, illustrated by Laura Cornell

# Implementing and Organizing Long-Term Studies

| | Art Installation | Infant Sibling or Young Pet Study | Construction Project | Natural Object Observation |
|---|---|---|---|---|
| **Obtain Permission** | From your administrators | From children's parents/guardians | From your administrator to leave the grounds, if necessary | From your administrator to leave the grounds, if necessary |
| **Implementation Timeline** | Weekly or monthly | Monthly or bimonthly | Weekly, bi-weekly, or monthly | Monthly |
| **Documentation** | • Photos<br>• Discussions<br>• Observational notes and drawings | • Photos<br>• Discussions<br>• Observational notes (about changes in hair, size, etc.) and drawings<br>• Charts measuring height (using unit blocks, LEGO bricks, or measuring tapes) | • Photos<br>• Discussions<br>• Observational notes and drawings | • Photos<br>• Discussions<br>• Observational notes and drawings |
| **Display Ideas** | Arrange a linear display that includes the children's writing and dictation, photos, and drawings. | Use a vertical display to show growth in height, including photos and written predictions of changes. | Arrange a display that includes the children's writing, photos, and drawings. | Arrange a display that includes the children's writing, photos, and drawings. |
| **High-Level Questions** | Look at this interesting art piece! Tell me what you see.<br><br>How could we add to our art installation?<br><br>What will happen if it rains?<br><br>How might other classes participate in our art installation? | How can you tell that Dylan's baby brother is growing?<br><br>What is different about Julian's kitten than when we saw her last month?<br><br>Let's measure the class turtle to see how much he has grown since we last measured him in October. | What do you see?<br><br>I wonder what they are building.<br><br>Do you see any materials that look like things we have in our classroom?<br><br>If we come back next week, how might it look different? | What do you know about this flower garden?<br><br>Let's predict what will happen to the leaves of this tree in autumn, winter, and spring.<br><br>What do you think we could learn if we visited this park all year? |

# Expand Children's Thinking and Learning by Asking Questions

**1** **Remember**
(identify, name, count, repeat, recall)

- How many toes does Adrianna's baby sister have?
- What color is the new house that is being built?
- What shape does this fence around the garden create?

**2** **Understand**
(describe, discuss, explain, summarize)

- Describe how the excavator picks up and moves the dirt.
- Explain what the architect added to the playground art area so that we could paint outside.
- What was the first (second, last) thing we added to the art installation?

**3** **Apply**
(explain why, dramatize, identify with/relate to)

- With your body, show how Adrianna's baby sister went from rolling over, to crawling, to standing, to toddling, and then finally to walking this year.
- Why do you think the architect chose to design the shopping center in that shape?
- What things in or around your house could you observe and make a change line for?

**4** **Analyze**
(recognize change, experiment, infer, compare, contrast)

- Put these photos in order of how the land looked before, during, and after the garden was completed.
- When you look at these photos of Adrianna's baby sister, what do you think she will look like and be able to do next year when she is 2 years old?
- How does the house look the same as (different from) the way it looked before it was renovated?

**5** **Evaluate**
(express opinion, judge, defend/criticize)

- Now that we have observed the maple tree all year, when do you think it looked the most beautiful? Why?
- What do you think were the most important changes you have seen in Adrianna's baby sister so far?
- What else could the architect add to the playground that you would really enjoy?

**6** **Create**
(make, construct, design, author)

- Make a picture (painting, construction) of what you predict the new building will look like.
- What materials could we use to make a mural to show how Adrianna's baby sister grows and changes? What would we put in the mural?
- How should we design our class book about watching our favorite maple tree change?

Down with convergent thinking and closed, absolute, right or wrong answers. Up with divergent thinking and open-ended exploring, brainstorming, wonder-full discussions and questions!

—Mimi Brodsky Chenfeld, *Still Teaching in the Key of Life: Joyful Stories From Early Childhood Settings*

# Using Featured Materials

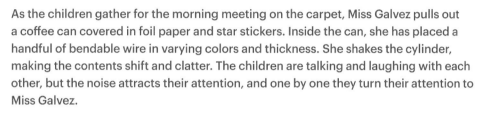

As the children gather for the morning meeting on the carpet, Miss Galvez pulls out a coffee can covered in foil paper and star stickers. Inside the can, she has placed a handful of bendable wire in varying colors and thickness. She shakes the cylinder, making the contents shift and clatter. The children are talking and laughing with each other, but the noise attracts their attention, and one by one they turn their attention to Miss Galvez.

"What's that?" 4-year-old Ruby asks, peering skeptically at the container. "It sounds all shaky and stuff."

Miss Galvez tells the class that inside the can is the new featured material that will be in the art area for a while. She begins by asking the children to describe what they are hearing. The children's eyes light up as they excitedly begin making guesses about the new material.

"It sounds like there's rocks inside!"

"It's like a maraca!"

As Miss Galvez sees their interest growing, she extends the learning further by asking them several higher-level questions. "What happens when I shake the box faster? How does the sound change? What do you think the featured material might be made of?"

Five-year-old Thanya points out, "It sounds different than the puffy balls," referring to a collection of pom-poms, the art area's featured material from a few months ago.

"Really? How is it different?" Miss Galvez asks.

Thanya is thoughtful, figuring out how to express the connection she has just made.

"Because this is a lot of noisy noise," suggests Ruby.

"Yeah!" Thanya exclaims. "The puffy balls wasn't noisy noise. It was little." She curls her body and lowers her voice, representing the "little" sound the cotton balls made.

Miss Galvez says, "Sounds like you're one step closer to guessing the new featured material!"

Thanya and Ruby giggle and high-five each other as the class continues to guess what is inside the can.

Young children are curious by nature, making the element of surprise a powerful tool for a teacher. A *featured material* is an interesting item that teachers can place in the classroom for a limited period of time, or for as long as the children remain intrigued by it. The material should be open ended (not have a set use or end result) and appeal to children's senses with a unique texture, shape, pattern, or color. In the opening scenario, the children's interest is piqued by the engaging way their teacher presents the new featured material.

In some ways, featured materials are similar to the materials described in Chapter 4 on makerspaces, and the notion that children experiment with these materials in their own way is related as well. However, featured materials offer children more opportunities to move items throughout the interest areas. In this way, they have the ability to compare and contrast the diverse possibilities of each material and use it for a variety of purposes.

Items to use as featured materials are almost limitless, but here are a few suggestions:

» Large pieces of textured fabric

» Unbreakable mirrors

» Multicolored cotton balls or pom-poms

» Smooth river stones

» Bendable wire of different thicknesses (cover any sharp edges with masking tape)

» Aluminum foil

» A collection of crystals and prisms in different shapes

## Getting Started

Think of new classroom materials as conversation starters and incorporate different levels of questions into interactions with the children when you introduce materials and during center time. When introducing a new material, hide the material in a paper bag and pass it around for the children to shake and feel. Or, as Miss Galvez did, manipulate it yourself. You can begin by asking lower-level questions like "What do you see (hear)?" and "What else sounds like this when you shake it (feels like this material in the bag)?" Then, you can support their higher-level thinking by asking "What do you think the featured material might be made of?," "Why?," and "How can we can get more clues about what the featured material is?"

Keep in mind that preschoolers and kindergartners may find it difficult to answer the highest levels of questions the first time you try this. As you continue to incorporate questioning into various parts of the day, their ability to think more complexly will develop over time. Helping children ponder and answer higher-level questions takes time and patience. As a teacher, you can often scaffold young learners from concrete thinking to more abstract thinking and support their use of expressive language. What is the foundation upon which all of this is built? Hands-on learning and real experiences with interesting materials.

## Supporting Children's Exploration and Learning

Including a featured material in each interest area is one way to begin focused lines of questioning with the children. For example, you can add smooth river stones in the dramatic play area, large pieces of textured fabric in the block area, aluminum foil in the art area, and small, multicolored tiles in the discovery area. After a material is introduced and the children have had opportunities to explore its properties, ask them to tell you what they notice: "How does that fabric feel to you?" and "What do you notice about these stones?" Start with Level 1 (Remembering) and Level 2 (Understanding) questions as appropriate, increasing the level of difficulty as the children's understanding grows. If children have commented on size, shape, or color, ask further questions about these characteristics, such as "What shape is this material?" or "Which of these is the biggest (smallest)?" Then, move on to more complex questions, such as "What do you think would happen if you put a piece of bendy wire here instead of the wood piece?" and "How can you move these pieces of Styrofoam around to transform this into something different?"

Once children have had ample opportunities to explore a material in one area, move the same material around the classroom and into different interest areas to encourage children to think about the material in different ways. You can even ask the children where else in the classroom they can use the material and how it might be used there. Record all the different ways you observe the children using it, places it is used the most, and what is the same or different about the way it is used in each area. When unbreakable mirrors were put in the discovery area next to a window of a mixed-age preschool classroom, the children held them up to the light and observed how the light reflected onto different parts of the room depending on which way they were turned. When the same mirrors were placed in the writing area, children were at first skeptical about how mirrors could be used there. After they began using dry-erase markers to write on them, however, the children commented on how the letters and shapes looked different than they did on paper. Asking simply, "How do they look different?" encouraged children to think deeper about their initial observations of the activity. While they peered into the mirrors and drew designs on their images, their teacher asked thoughtfully, "What happens to the writing and drawing when you move your reflection away from the mirror?" Teachers were able to ask high-level questions as the children gained a new perspective on a familiar material.

When young children see something that doesn't fit into the category that they expect, it is mysterious and exciting for them. This can help them come up with new ways to think about the material or concept. For example, if children find cotton balls in the art area, they may pick one up and begin stroking their face with it, as they have seen an adult do. But if the cotton balls are presented alongside paint or ink for stamping and the teacher asks the children how they might use the materials together, children have an opportunity to rework their understanding of how a cotton ball might fit in this new context.

To extend this approach further, exchange some materials with another classroom. Present the selected material to the other class and say, "We are exploring all the different ways this can be used. We would like you to help us out with this project by writing down what you see and do with it." Or, to bring higher-level vocabulary in, you can say something like, "We would like you to help us with our *research*. We want to *compare* all the different *functions* of this *material*. Will you *document* your *observations* of how your class uses it?"

## The Picture Book Connection

*Hannah's Collections*, by Marthe Jocelyn

*Not a Box*, by Antoinette Portis

*Not a Stick*, by Antoinette Portis

*Regards to the Man in the Moon*, by Ezra Jack Keats

*Roxaboxen*, by Alice McLerran, illustrated by Barbara Cooney

While a well-stocked classroom is essential to creating a developmentally appropriate environment for preschoolers and kindergartners, it is important to remember that meaning is not in the materials, it is in the mind. A single featured material used in a variety of thoughtful ways offers countless opportunities for high-level questions and conversations with young children. When you start with interesting materials, introducing them to children in ways that inspire their curiosity will keep them engaged and learning.

# Expand Children's Thinking and Learning by Asking Questions

**1** **Remember**
(identify, name, count, repeat, recall)

- What is this material called?
- How many pieces of wire do you have?
- What color are these stones?

**2** **Understand**
(describe, discuss, explain, summarize)

- Tell me how you got the foil to make this shape. What did you do first (next)?
- Describe how the prism feels in your hand.
- How did you use the mirror when it was in the art area?

**3** **Apply**
(explain why, dramatize, identify with/relate to)

- What are some other ways you could use these longer pieces of wire?
- Why do you think you weren't able to attach this piece of velvet fabric to your collage?
- Where else have you seen this kind of prism?

**4** **Analyze**
(recognize change, experiment, infer, compare, contrast)

- Now that the pieces of fabric are in the dramatic play area, do you use them differently than the way you used them in the art area?
- How did the stones change when you put them into the water table?
- What is the same (different) about all of these prisms and crystals?

**5** **Evaluate**
(express opinion, judge, defend/criticize)

- Which fabric did you like working with the most in the art area? Why?
- What was your favorite way to use the foil? Why?
- What could you do to the wire so that it stays around the playdough better?

**6** **Create**
(make, construct, design, author)

- I see you're using the counting bears in the discovery area today. I wonder if you can make something with these longer wire pieces that could hold some of the bears.
- How can you use these colorful cotton balls to make something that we can hang from the ceiling or put on the wall?
- Let's write a story about all the different ways we used the stones in the classroom.

Train yourself to ask yourself (and the children you work with), "What else?" No matter what you're doing, thinking, or planning, whisper, "What else?" to yourself, and your brain will begin whirling. What else can we add to this idea? What else can we combine? What else will connect?

—Mimi Brodsky Chenfeld, *Still Teaching in the Key of Life: Joyful Stories From Early Childhood Settings*

# Multiday Explorations

**16**

Mrs. Hodge's small group table is covered with recyclables and "junk"—empty plastic water bottles and caps, cardboard boxes of various sizes, wire hangers, old combs, poker chips, paper towel rolls, straws, and fabric squares. Her small group, which includes 4- and 5-year-old children of varying levels of ability, is busy at work on 3-D art creations. It is the second day of a multiday exploration, and the children are working on the creations they started the day before.

Mrs. Hodge turns to her right and says, "It looks like you've done some more work on your invention, Stacia. Yesterday, you told me you were making a house-car. I see you added wheels today. What other changes have you made?"

Stacia looks at her creation thoughtfully and points to several pom-poms attached to the front of the structure with tape. "I put the lights in the front."

On the other end of the table, Kymm and Jackson are working side by side. Kymm says, "This big part looks the same—like yours!" She points to a straw sticking out of the top of her invention, then to a straw glued to the side of Jackson's. Mrs. Hodge notes Kymm's observation and reminds herself to ask Kymm in what other ways the two creations are similar.

Lexie taps Mrs. Hodge on the shoulder and says, "Remember I was trying to hang the cans from the wire so they would bump into each other and make a jingly noise like the chimes we have hanging on the playground? Well, I did it! I used the tape my daddy gave us from his workshop. I asked him to help me figure out a way to do it when I couldn't get the cans to stay on the wire the way I wanted."

Later, when Mrs. Hodge changes the mobile in their play area, the children can compare the sounds made by the two different mobiles, and Mrs. Hodge can ask some guiding questions to help the children think about why. She wonders if this might be the beginning of a unit on mobiles!

Small group activities that extend over several days offer children opportunities to take part in planning, creating, and reflecting—all part of the creative process. Using a carefully planned framework, you can incorporate mini-studies on topics that are interesting and relevant to the children and that provide opportunities for in-depth learning.

## Getting Started

Some materials that work well for multiday small group explorations include

» **Recyclables and "junk":** cardboard tubes, empty tissue boxes, bottle caps, Styrofoam pieces, and straws

» **Playdough and natural materials:** twigs, leaves, small stones, sprigs of lavender and eucalyptus, pinecones, and seed pods

» **Carpentry materials**: small wood pieces, carpet squares, upholstery fabric, wallpaper samples, mosaic tiles, wood flooring scraps, acrylic plastic pieces, small dowels, and decorative wooden accents

Provide a variety of connectors for children to affix one material to another while constructing, such as various types of tape (electrical, masking, painter's), staplers and staples, glue, binder clips, and small brads. "Break-apart" tools such as child-size safety scissors, hole punchers, and plastic knives are also important items to include when planning for a multiday exploration. If you send home a note to families asking for donations, you will be amazed at what you can get! Provide examples of the types of materials you are looking for and why you are collecting them. Check to see whether your community has a creative reuse center. These centers offer affordable reusable materials from business and individual donations, like art supplies, paper, fabric, and bulk items, that teachers can use for art activities, makerspace projects, and other creative pursuits.

The table on pages 109–110 shows examples of the kinds of things you can do during each day of a three-day exploration.

## Day-to-Day Instructions and Questions

| | Instructions | Questions |
|---|---|---|
| **Day 1** | • Introduce materials and explore their actual and possible uses with the children.<br><br>• Provide a tray or cardboard to use as a base, and encourage the children to begin examining, sorting, and playing with the materials while you talk about them.<br><br>• Take a "before" photo of the children exploring the materials. | • "What is this material?" (Level 1)<br><br>• "Describe this collection of materials you've chosen." (Level 2)<br><br>• "Why did you pick this material to be part of your creation?" (Level 3)<br><br>• "Why do you think this tape is going to be strong enough to hold these two pieces of plastic together?" (Level 5) |
| **Day 2** | • Distribute any creations (structures, inventions, contraptions) from the previous day, if the children have gotten that far. (If not, just put the materials out again.)<br><br>• (Optional step) If appropriate, have children create observational drawings of their work up to this point. Discuss the drawings with the children, and encourage the children to also discuss them with each other.<br><br>• Discuss the changes they want to make.<br><br>• Give each child a plastic baggie and invite the children to go to the art area to gather the materials they need to carry out their plans. You can accompany them to remind them of their task. Collect the baggies and place them in small group time baskets for the next day. | • "How is your creation different from yesterday?" (Level 4)<br><br>• "What was the hardest part of putting all of the materials together?" (Level 5)<br><br>• "You say you want to add seats to your airplane. What kind of seat will you design with these materials?" (Level 6)<br><br>• "What do you think you might want to add or change tomorrow?" (Level 6) |
| **Day 3** | • Distribute the in-progress creations again, along with the baggies from the previous day and other art supplies.<br><br>• Remind children of the plans they made the previous day. Continue to ask questions throughout the process.<br><br>• Encourage children to ask each other questions and assist each other with problems they encounter with materials.<br><br>• Label creations in more detail and take an "after" photo of the work at the end of small group time. | • "What do you notice about your friends' creations that are the same as (different from) yours?" (Level 4)<br><br>• "What other materials would you have liked to add if we had them?" (Level 5)<br><br>• "If you were going to start all over again, what would you do differently this time?" (Level 5)<br><br>• "Let's write a story about how you made your invention over the last few days." (Level 6)<br><br>• "Ask your friends a question about their creations." (Offer suggestions of questions to ask if the child is new to the concept of asking questions.) (Level 6) |

*continued on next page*

| | Instructions | Questions |
|---|---|---|
| **Follow-up and Reflection** | • Reflect with the children on the changes that took place on the work on the first, second, and third days, and discuss the process of how the changes happened.<br>• Create a documentation board of the exploration with each child's before and after photos, dictations, and observational drawings.<br>• Do classroom walk-throughs with the children, and refer back to the work on display. | • "How does your contraption look different now from when you started?" (Level 4)<br>• "How did other children use the materials you used? Was it in the same way or different?" (Level 4)<br>• "What did you learn about the materials you worked with?" (Level 5) |

Multiday explorations allow children to observe change over time, revise their ideas and their creations, and reflect on the change process and their own thinking. Asking children questions as they plan, create, and reflect is a great way to support their thinking and learning!

## Supporting Children's Exploration and Learning

Offer new or familiar materials and encourage children to explore their potential uses. (For more on using new materials, see Chapter 15, Using Featured Materials. Also see Chapter 4 for materials and exploration in classroom makerspaces.) This is one example of introducing abstract ways of thinking to more concrete thinkers. Don't be afraid to use complicated words like *structure*, *contraption*, or *invention*. Along with expanding children's vocabularies, it also adds an element of excitement for young children to hear their work described using sophisticated words.

Working on a creation for several days gives you and the children a chance to slow down and discuss what they are doing at various stages over time. As in the vignette above, children become very involved in their creative ideas. They have time to come up with solutions to problems, share what they are doing with their families, and change and improve their ideas to make the abstract become concrete. Ask good questions to support the exploration of the materials and planning during the first day, during the actual construction of the creations, on the second and third days, and after the creations have been completed. When you ask questions to guide these activities, progressing from basic to more complex questions, you support children's creativity and higher-level thinking.

## Boosting Vocabulary

| Instead of saying . . . | Try saying . . . |
| --- | --- |
| "Today we are making . . ." | "Today is the first day of our exploration!" |
| "What did you make?" | "Tell me about this part of your creation (structure, contraption)." |
| "Are you done?" | "Tonight, think about what you might like to add or change tomorrow." |
| "This part is not working. Here's how you fix it." | "What can you do to get this part to work the way you want?" |

## The Picture Book Connection

*Balancing Act,* by Ellen Stoll Walsh

*Cubes, Cones, Cylinders, & Spheres,* by Tana Hoban

*Dreaming Up: A Celebration of Building,* by Christy Hall

*Perfect Square,* by Michael Hall

*What Do Wheels Do All Day?* by April Jones Prince, illustrated by Giles Laroche

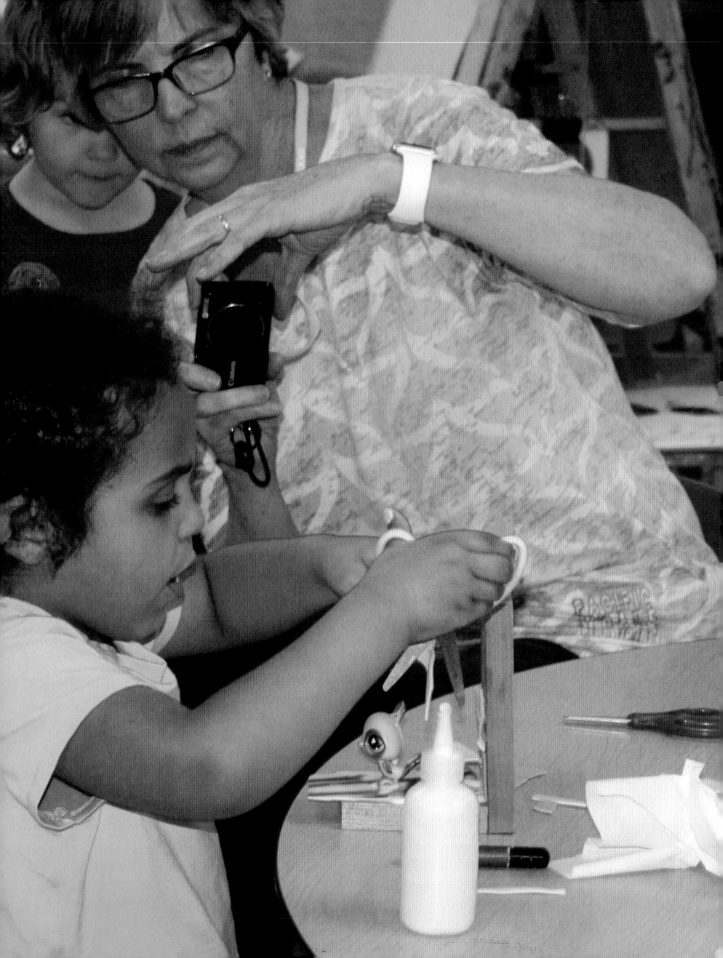

# Expand Children's Thinking and Learning by Asking Questions

**1 Remember**
(identify, name, count, repeat, recall)

- What colors are you using in your creation?
- How many bottle caps did you use?
- What is the name of this material?

**2 Understand**
(describe, discuss, explain, summarize)

- Where do you think this box (can, cardboard cylinder) came from?
- How did you attach all of these pinecones and lavender sprigs to your creation?
- Describe how you changed the shapes of these tissue boxes to make your creation.

**3 Apply**
(explain why, dramatize, identify with/relate to)

- Explain why you decided to use only the leaves, sprigs, and twigs for your creation.
- How do you think other people could use what you created?
- If you were going to display your creation in your house, where would you put it? Why would you choose that spot?

**4 Analyze**
(recognize change, experiment, infer, compare, contrast)

- How did your creation change from yesterday?
- What is the same (different) about the way you used the twigs and leaves and the way your friend used these same materials?
- How will you have to change your creation so that those pipe cleaners and mosaic tiles will stick on the way you want?

**5 Evaluate**
(express opinion, judge, defend/criticize)

- How do you feel about your creation?
- Is it exactly the way you want it to be, or do you have some ideas about how you want to change it?
- Which part of your invention do you like the best? What was your favorite part about making it?

**6 Create**
(make, construct, design, author)

- Let's give your creation a title (name) and tell a little imaginary story about it. What do you want to call it?
- What would you like to write (dictate for me to write) about your creation for our photo caption on the documentation board?
- How can you design something that will hold your creation in place on the shelf so it doesn't fall off and that will keep your friends from touching it?

It is not our differences that divide us. It is our inability to recognize, accept, and celebrate those differences.

—Audre Lorde, *Our Dead Behind Us: Poems*

# Supporting Children's Understanding About Diversity

Ranita Cheruvu

The children in Ms. Talia's kindergarten classroom are eagerly awaiting the visitors for their family traditions museum. The children have been learning all about each other's family backgrounds, languages, and traditions, and they have created exhibits about them. The classroom is filled with the voices of excited children and artifacts from their families. At one table, Theo starts sharing his family tradition with Ms. Lina, a classmate's aunt.

After he explains about Friday night dinners and game night at his poppa's house, he asks Ms. Lina, "How come you speak English like me?"

Ms. Lina smiles and replies, "Why wouldn't I speak English like you?"

Theo pauses and then says, "'Cause you look like Ariel's mommy, and she doesn't speak English good and it sounds funny."

Across the room, two children from the classroom next door stop by Maya's table and start looking at her pictures and a blanket from her exhibit. Maya explains that her special blanket was made from Indian saris belonging to the women in her mother's family.

As she shows the pictures of her family, Simone asks Maya, "How come your mommy and daddy don't match? Your mommy has brown skin, and your daddy has white skin. That's weird. My mommy and daddy both have white skin."

These interactions in Ms. Talia's classroom are nothing out of the ordinary. They represent the many ways that young children make sense of the various aspects of human diversity that surrounds them.

The term *diversity* is often used to refer to people who look, speak, or act in ways that are different from what is considered the societal norm. A more inclusive view of diversity suggests that it is part of the natural order of human existence, that the multiple ways people look, speak, and act are all beautiful and normal. This view focuses on celebrating the numerous lifestyles humans have in the world and appreciating the ways diversity enriches our human experience. While some people think that teachers need to focus on the ways that people are similar, many multicultural educators agree that it is only when people understand and appreciate diversity that they can truly understand how we are similar (Derman-Sparks & Edwards 2010; Ramsey 2015).

As racial, cultural, and linguistic diversity in the United States continues to expand, young children are more likely than past generations to see people who do not look, speak, or act like them. Through their countless observations and interactions, children are always applying what they already understand about human diversity, and then either confirming or adapting what they know. In the opening vignette, both Theo and Simone are applying their emerging understandings of ethnicity, language, race, and family. Theo assumes that Ms. Lina would speak English with a Dominican accent like Ariel's mother because Theo thinks that Ms. Lina looks Latina. This assumption is based on his understanding of what makes someone Latina in terms of how she looks and sounds. Theo has not yet developed an understanding that Latinos are a diverse group, that they can be fluent in English, Spanish, Portuguese, and other languages to varying degrees, and that some Latinos might speak English with an American accent. Simone also makes assumptions about families and race. Based on her prior understandings, she assumes that members of a family must be of the same race and therefore have the same skin color. In both instances, Theo and Simone are presented with information that does not fit into their existing understanding of human diversity. Their questions are evidence that they are trying to reconcile this new information with what they already know.

## Getting Started

When children make comments such as Theo's and Simone's, some adults respond by telling them "Don't say that," or "That's not nice." In other cases, adults might explain what is wrong about their comments. In both of these responses, children are being *told* about diversity rather than being supported to reach a new understanding—the understanding that people within and across various racial, cultural, and linguistic groups do not all look, think, speak, and act the same. Good teaching practices tell us that children learn best when they are given opportunities to construct their ideas, and the same logic holds true for how you can support children's perspectives of diversity with high-level questions. Rather than merely telling children about diversity, allow them to express their ideas and then help them reach a new understanding about the richness of human diversity by asking thought-provoking questions.

## Supporting Children's Learning

Children need learning experiences and opportunities that help them develop an understanding of diversity as the norm. This can be accomplished in several ways that build on one another:

» Provide experiences that help children develop positive individual and group identities. It is only when children appreciate their own racial, cultural, and language backgrounds that they can learn to appreciate the backgrounds of other people around them.

» Use classroom materials (e.g., books, dolls, figurines, visual aids, and art) that represent people from diverse racial, cultural, and linguistic backgrounds.

» Avoid stereotypical representations of groups (such as Native Americans in teepees) in lessons and classroom materials.

» Provide experiences and materials (such as a wall of children's family photos) that allow children to see that there is diversity even within a particular racial, cultural, and linguistic group.

» Balance celebrating diversity with unity by pointing out both the commonalities and differences across shared human experiences, such as how birthdays are celebrated.

» Infuse diversity into all aspects of the daily classroom routine, environment, and activities, and not just as a special lesson or unit. For example, notice and discuss the different types of styles, colors, and textures of hair among children in the class, or the variety of languages spoken by the people in your school. As children make observations and ask questions that relate to issues of diversity, use these teachable moments to address their questions and talk about their ideas.

» Provide opportunities for children to interact with people from a wide range of racial, cultural, and linguistic backgrounds by reaching out to colleagues, friends, families, and local community members.

Ms. Talia uses some of these strategies for the family traditions project described in the vignette. She has the children work with their families to identify their own traditions. The class then learns about their classmates' traditions, like names, recipes, vacations, and heirlooms. During the project, Ms. Talia reads stories about family traditions that include characters from many different backgrounds, such as *The Relatives Came*, by Cynthia Rylant, illustrated by Stephen Gammell; *I Love Saturdays y domingos*, by Alma Flor Ada, illustrated by Elivia Savadier; and *The Granddaughter Necklace,* by Sharon Dennis Wyeth, illustrated by Bagram Ibatoulline. These collective experiences show the children that there are many types of family traditions and that each one is equally and uniquely enriching to families.

Although Ms. Talia has a classroom that celebrates diversity, there is a continuous need to observe and respond to the children's inquiries and assumptions about human diversity. Based on Theo's comments to Ms. Lina, Ms. Talia knows that she needs to provide the children in her class with materials and learning experiences that show that there are multiple ways to be Latina. By asking high-level questions such as "What are some ways that you are similar to and different from your friend Kendrick [another African American boy in the class]?" and discussing children's ideas, she can highlight that, among many other differences across Latino cultures, not all Latinos speak English, Spanish, Portuguese, and other languages the same way.

Let's imagine that Ms. Talia witnessed Maya and Simone's interaction. She knows that many of the children in her class come from monoracial, monolingual, and monocultural families, and she wants to use this opportunity to expand the children's understandings of diversity and families.

> The following day, Ms. Talia asks during the class meeting, "What were some of the exhibits at our family traditions museum? What is a family tradition?"
> (Level 1: Remember).
>
> The children recall and share their responses, such as "One of my favorite exhibits was Maya's blanket. It reminded me of the quilt that my grandmother made for me when I was a baby."
>
> "Did anyone else notice anything that is similar to something in their family?" questions Ms. Talia (Level 3: Apply). Later in the conversation, she adds, "Simone, I noticed that you also visited Maya's exhibit. Please describe her family tradition to us. Why is it considered a tradition?" (Level 3: Apply).
>
> After Simone explains that Maya's blanket is made from Indian saris, Ms. Talia asks, "Simone, you noticed something about Maya's mother and father. Explain to our class what you noticed in her pictures and what you asked her," (Level 3: Apply). Simone responds, and the teacher summarizes her explanation. "So Simone noticed that Maya's mom is Indian and has brown skin, and her dad is Italian and has peach-colored skin. She said that they don't look the same and was wondering why. Simone, why was that surprising to you?" (Level 2: Understand).

Simone answers that everyone's skin in her family matches. Ms. Talia says, "Hmm, you know what? This reminds me of when we studied our families. One of the things we talked about was who was in our family, and we made a graph of the number of people in our family. Let me go get that so we can look at it."

After she displays the graph, she asks the children, "What does our graph tell us about families?" (Level 4: Analyze). A child responds that all families are different and have a different number of people in them. "Yes, all families are different. One way they're different is in how many people are in the family. In what other ways are families different?" (Level 3: Apply).

The class shares several responses, and Ms. Talia expands on these by reminding them of family similarities and differences based on the diverse traditions they saw in their family tradition museum exhibits.

"Now let's go back to Simone's question about whether or not families have to have matching skin color. We can look at our class book on our families to see if we can figure out the answer to that question," says Ms. Talia. As she flips through the pages with photographs, she asks children to make observations about the people in their families. She stops in between to ask, "In what ways are our families similar? In what ways are they different?" (Level 4: Analyze). Next, she asks them each to look closely at their family photo and decide if their family members all have the same skin color (Level 4: Analyze).

Ms. Talia wants the children to move to an understanding that families can look and act very differently. She thinks about how she can help them create a more

inclusive definition of families as a circle of people who love and care for one another.

With this in mind, the next day she asks the children, "How might it feel if someone told you that your family is strange or not a real family? Why would you feel that way?" (Level 5: Evaluate). After the children share their responses and agree that it would be hurtful, she reads a modified definition of *family* from the *Merriam-Webster Dictionary* to the class. "'A family is a group of individuals living under one roof and usually with one person in charge.' What do you think about this definition? Does it include your family? Whose family might it leave out?"(Level 5: Evaluate).

Given the children's responses, she tells the class that they are going to make their own definition that includes all families. As a group, the class shares ideas about what the definition should include (Level 6: Create). After creating a list, they evaluate each idea to make sure it is fair and doesn't leave anyone out (Level 5: Evaluate). Once the children create a common definition, they draw pictures of their own families and dictate to Ms. Talia why their families are special and what makes them a family (Level 6: Create).

As you work with children to deepen and expand their understanding of diversity, higher-level questioning and critical thinking are essential. The questions you ask must build on what students know and have experienced. Find a balance between guiding the conversation with respect to diversity and engaging in discussions that are responsive to what children are saying and seeing. Be flexible and slow down the pace as needed. It is also important to use high-level questions and cognitive learning experiences continuously throughout the year. Through our commitment to providing opportunities that *show* children that diversity is all around them and a natural part of human existence, children can develop a true appreciation and understanding of the richness of the world in which they live. If appreciation and understanding of diversity are cultivated from a young age, it will translate into empathy and compassion for others, whether we are the same or different (Souto-Manning 2013).

## The Picture Book Connection

*All the Colors We Are/Todos los colores de nuestra piel,* by Katie Kissinger, photographs by Wernher Krutein

*And Tango Makes Three,* by Justin Richardson and Peter Parnell, illustrated by Henry Cole

*Apple Pie 4th of July,* by Janet S. Wong, illustrated by Margaret Chodos-Irvine

*Last Stop on Market Street,* by Matt de la Peña, illustrated by Christian Robinson

*Moses Goes to a Concert,* by Isaac Millman

# Expand Children's Thinking and Learning by Asking Questions

## 1 Remember
(identify, name, count, repeat, recall)

- What are some ways we can say *friend* in other languages?
- Think of a time when someone teased you because you looked different from them. How did it make you feel?
- What holidays do we celebrate as a class?

## 2 Understand
(describe, discuss, explain, summarize)

- How would you describe the oldest living person in your family? Tell me about something special that person can do.
- How would you describe what is beautiful about your hair?
- How does a person who is deaf communicate?

## 3 Apply
(explain why, dramatize, identify with/relate to)

- Think about how you feel when you celebrate Hanukkah or Christmas. Why might a friend celebrating Diwali also be excited about their celebration?
- Why are all family traditions special?
- Why do you think some boys might feel shy or worried to play with dolls?

## 4 Analyze
(recognize change, experiment, infer, compare, contrast)

- What are some similarities between you and Charlie from the book *My Brother Charlie* (by Holly Robinson Peete and Ryan Elizabeth Peete, illustrated by Shane W. Evans)?
- How would you feel if your friends wouldn't let you play with them on the swings because you look or speak differently than them?
- Let's look at our books on scientists and athletes. How many of them feature boys, and how many feature girls? What do you think about that difference?

## 5 Evaluate
(express opinion, judge, defend/criticize)

- In the book we read, children with brown skin were not allowed to attend the same school as children with light color skin. Why was this fair or unfair?
- In the book *Something Beautiful* (by Sharon Dennis Wyeth, illustrated by Chris K. Soentpiet) the girl found some beautiful things about her neighborhood and some things she wanted to change. What are some beautiful things about your neighborhood and some things you want to change?
- What do you think makes someone a good friend (president)? If you were choosing a friend (voting), what kind of characteristics would you look for?

## 6 Create
(make, construct, design, author)

- How can we redesign our classroom so that it is easier for a friend who uses a wheelchair to move around?
- How would you redesign the packaging on your favorite toy so that either a boy or a girl would want to play with it?
- Make a page for our class book that explains what makes your friend beautiful.

The environment should act as a kind of aquarium, which reflects the ideas, ethics, attitudes and cultures of the people who live in it. This is what we are working toward.

—Loris Malaguzzi, *Working in the Reggio Way: A Beginner's Guide for American Teachers*

# Making the Most of Classroom Displays

**18**

Ms. Melisano's mixed-age preschool class is busy at work during center time when the program's director, Mr. Bat-Ami, and assistant director enter the room. They greet the teachers and children and begin glancing around the room.

"We are here to do a walk-through," Mr. Bat-Ami announces. "We want to see all of the wonderful things you've been working on!"

The children watch the adults curiously. They take notes and peer closely at the displays of the children's work on the walls.

Four-year-old Jennah approaches the director and says, "That's mine, you know. See my name and this blue bumpy part over here? That's my picture of the hardware store."

The pair chats about the drawing, and other children eagerly point out their own drawings and writing displayed around the room. Ms. Melisano smiles and decides to talk to the children about walk-throughs at the end of the day.

Most preschool and kindergarten classrooms are filled with children's artwork and writing—paintings and stories displayed on the walls, mobiles hanging from the ceiling, and LEGO structures and descriptions standing on a display shelf. According to resources and evaluation instruments such as the *Early Childhood Environment Rating Scale,* Third Edition (ECERS-3), it is essential to carefully select children's artwork and intentionally interact with children about what is displayed (Harms, Clifford, & Cryer 2014). These interactions can include everything from one-to-one conversations with a child to reading aloud the words in displays in ways that are engaging for children.

By guiding children in discussions about their displayed work, early childhood educators are using one of the most powerful teaching resources they possess—the classroom itself. The classroom environment is often referred to as "the third teacher" (Carter 2007), and displays of children's work are a significant part of that. Preschoolers and kindergartners are exposed to and, ideally, interacting with their environment on a daily basis.

## Getting Started

Just as you are mindful of the language you choose to use with children and the questions you ask, thoughtfully select and arrange children's work. Often, the phrase "less is more" applies to classroom environments. Do your own walk-through of your classroom, and consider these questions as you look around:

» Do the many items on the walls distract you?

» Are materials stacked on top of shelves in a way that is messy, distracting, or unsafe?

» Does each child's work look almost identical, or are the creations unique?

» Is the children's work displayed at their eye level?

» Do the children have the opportunity to provide input on what, where, and how their work is displayed?

» Are there shelves or tables to display children's 3-D art (sculptures, clay creations, etc.)?

» Are children's 2-D works matted or framed in cardboard, recycled, or donated frames to make them look special?

» Do you change what is displayed often, or is the same work displayed for long periods of time?

Asking yourself these questions is a key step in creating an environment that inspires, interests, and teaches.

## Supporting Children's Learning

To maximize the educational potential of the environment, take students around the room as a whole group or in small groups and point out the displays. Make sure each child has at least one piece of work he can talk about, ask the children low- and high-level questions about their work, and reflect on the finished and in-progress work displayed on the walls or shelves.

You can also hold small group discussions about the displays during mealtimes and transitions. Begin a lunchtime conversation by casually pointing to a display and saying, "Remember when we made those drawings? I see someone drew a hammer with a big handle, and here someone glued craft sticks on their paper in a long row. What do you remember about this work and why we did it?" Discuss the children's prior learning and the details of the work. This activity lends itself to every level of questioning, from the simplest to the most complex. For example, here are some questions you might ask children about the work they created after a visit to the local hardware store:

» **Level 1 (Remember):** "How many shopping carts did you draw?"

» **Level 2 (Understand):** "Tell us how you used these LEGO bricks to show the front of the store."

- » **Level 3 (Apply):** "When you look at your work all around the room, what else do you remember about our field trip?"
- » **Level 4 (Analyze):** "Let's read the words we wrote next to your painting of the woodworking section of the store. What other work have you created in the classroom that reminds you of the woodworking section?"
- » **Level 5 (Evaluate):** Tell me about your favorite part of this collage you made out of paint samples from the store."
- » **Level 6 (Create):** "What can we title our mural about our trip to the hardware store?"

Having children create individualized artwork plays a primary role in how many teachable moments you will uncover as students interact with their "third teacher." Children should not only be able to identify their own work, they should also be confident in their own abilities without having to compare them to another child's.

Consider what your displays and bulletin boards look like to the children and their families. If children are creating flowers, is each child's different? Are they using materials of their own choice in their own way? If you give the children a model or tell them which materials to use to make something, their creativity is limited and each child's work will look the

same. Your questions will likely be lower-level ones ("What color is this leaf?" and "How many petals does your flower have?"), and your ability to prompt children to think more deeply about their process and evaluate their own efforts will be restricted. Constructions should represent children's individual creative expression, not how well they can follow directions.

By displaying individualized art, you open the door for high-level questions and discussions around the work. You enable the children to take ownership of their own creations, and you also set the stage for positive conversations with families about their child's work. Perhaps most important, during these discussions you have opportunities to meet each child at her developmental level and scaffold her learning.

## The Picture Book Connection

*The Dot*, by Peter H. Reynolds

*Henri's Scissors*, by Jeanette Winter

*The Looking Book*, by P.K. Hallinan, illustrated by Patrice Barton

*The Museum*, by Susan Verde, illustrated by Peter H. Reynolds

*Museum Trip,* by Barbara Lehman

### More Ways to Use Classroom Displays to Support High-Level Thinking

Encourage a more complex, reflective line of questioning by asking children to compare and/or contrast these displayed items:

- A photo of a child creating a piece next to the piece itself
- Photos of an object over a period of time, displayed in a linear fashion (For more on this idea, see Chapter 14, "Kickstarting the School Year: Exploring Change Through Long-Term Studies.")
- Photos of a 3-D structure next to the structure itself, taken from several different angles (head on, above, behind)
- Two similar pieces of work created by the same child a few months apart, such as self-portraits or invented spelling attempts

For more ideas on documenting and displaying children's work, see Chapter 19, "Documenting Children's Learning."

# Expand Children's Thinking and Learning by Asking Questions

**1** **Remember**
(identify, name, count, repeat, recall)

- How many colors of paint did you use in this painting?
- What is this material called?
- What tools did you use to create this sculpture?

**2** **Understand**
(describe, discuss, explain, summarize)

- Tell me how you attached the sponge pieces to your paper.
- How did you move the block structure from the carpet to this shelf?
- What ideas did your group come up with to include in our display of the trip to the car wash?

**3** **Apply**
(explain why, dramatize, identify with/relate to)

- How did you attach this painting to the side of the shelf?
- Show me with your hands how you made this shape with the paintbrush. How about this other shape?
- Show us some of the things that a bus driver does that you learned from our study of school buses.

**4** **Analyze**
(recognize change, experiment, infer, compare, contrast)

- Look at these two drawings of yours. What is different about your name on each one?
- Why do you think this pom-pom fell off your collage? How could you reattach it?
- What materials do you think would work best for your idea?

**5** **Evaluate**
(express opinion, judge, defend/criticize)

- How do you feel about the color you got when you mixed those two paints together?
- Where would be the best place to hang this so your grandma can see it when she picks you up today? Why?
- Look at Rafael's drawing. What do you suppose he was thinking about when he made it?

**6** **Create**
(make, construct, design, author)

- This design you made with LEGO bricks is interesting. Do you think you could make the same design with wooden blocks? Why would or wouldn't it look the same?
- Now that we've visited a construction site, what can we add to this class story we wrote about our trip to the hardware store? What details could you add that you didn't know before?
- Since you think it is important for the family to be really quiet in the dramatic play area when the baby is trying to sleep, how can you make a sign to display that reminds everyone about that?

Through documentation the teacher can make it possible for others to "see" the learning that takes place when developmentally appropriate teaching occurs.

—Judy Harris Helm, Sallee Beneke, and Kathy Steinheimer, *Windows on Learning: Documenting Young Children's Work*, Second Edition

# Documenting Children's Learning

Cindy Gennarelli

During morning center time, 4-year-old Azizi is working with markers on the whiteboard. His classmate, Madison, is sitting off to the side watching him very intently. She is using a crayon to make marks on a piece of paper attached to a clipboard. As Ms. Grace walks closer to Madison, she motions with her hand, indicating that Ms. Grace should sit next to her.

Madison puts her finger to her lips. "Ms. Grace, come here and sit down next to me, but please be quiet. See, I am very busy writing things down like you do. I don't want to miss anything Azizi is doing because he is doing very, very important stuff."

Ms. Grace quietly nods and then softly says, "Okay, tell me if there is anything that you would like me to do."

"Maybe you can use your fancy camera and take some pictures while I write," Madison does not hesitate to respond. "This is just so great, and I don't want to miss anything." She approaches Azizi as soon as he completes his drawing. "I noticed you were very busy concentrating on your work. I wonder what you can tell me about your drawing."

Azizi turns to the teacher. "Ms. Grace, did you take photos of everything that I did?"

"Yes, she did, Azizi," Madison quickly replies. "I told her to take pictures. See? Ms. Grace is already putting them on the computer. Let's look at them, Azizi. You can tell me everything." Madison starts pointing to the photos. "Oh, this is very interesting. What would you like to tell me about your drawing?"

Looking only at the final photo, Azizi tells the story of the truck he drew, which belongs to his dad. Then he lets Ms. Grace know he is done at the whiteboard. Both Azizi and Madison move on to other interest areas. Ms. Grace prints the photos and begins to put together a documentation panel for Azizi's work that includes his story. She plans to revisit the photos with Azizi later in the day and ask additional follow-up questions.

Documentation is how educators make a child's learning visible. It tells a story of children's learning so you and the child can understand her thoughts and interests. It looks different for every child and is most authentic when children are engaged in simple everyday experiences. Families have the opportunity to see and read about their children's day when documentation panels are placed in the hallways and on bulletin boards outside the classroom. By asking children appropriate questions about what they are doing, you can learn a great deal about them, help them revisit their activities, and share their learning with their families and others. In the vignette above, Madison has learned from watching her teacher what it is like to deeply observe the work of another student. She is exploring the role of playing teacher, mimicking the actions and language Ms. Grace models for the children.

The Reggio Emilia approach to learning has contributed a great deal to educators' understanding about the value of documentation. According to Loris Malaguzzi, founder of the Reggio Emilia schools, children "become even more curious, interested, and confident as they contemplate the meaning of what they have achieved" (1993, 63).

## Getting Started

Documentation can happen frequently and in such a positive way that in a class like Ms. Grace's, you often hear children telling adults, "Come quick, you have to see this and write down everything that we're doing!" You can capture children's positive learning experiences throughout the day, during large and small group meetings, center time, snack and lunch time, and outdoor time. Children should be comfortable with the types of questions you ask and feel empowered by the constructive feedback you can offer. When speaking with children about their work, embed open-ended questions as part of an informal conversation. Avoid providing an answer or assuming that you know what the children are doing before they tell you.

What and how you document should always be natural, not staged. Watch for and document the ordinary moments of learning rather than a situation you set up specifically for the purpose of documenting. Documentation experiences should be as unique as each child. Ask yourself why you are documenting the experience. Is it because you see a child perform a task for the first time, or perhaps more skillfully than ever before? Do you notice something in a child's behavior that gives you insight into growth in his development? Has a child used a new word or expressed understanding of a new concept?

Here are some suggestions for documenting a child's learning:

» Capture children engaging in genuine child-directed learning experiences.

» Record what a child is saying and doing by writing a brief anecdote or description.

» Take photos of what the child is doing. (When possible, keep a camera nearby.)

» Leave notepaper in baskets around the room for easy access.

» If you see or hear something interesting, write it down and decide later if it is significant enough to warrant becoming a part of a more formal assessment of the child.

» Have informal conversations with children. Ask clarifying questions to help you understand their thinking about what they're doing.

» Create a documentation panel that chronicles children's in-depth study of a topic, including the steps involved throughout the study.

## Supporting Children's Learning

Azizi is so proud to see that Ms. Grace places the documentation panel about his work in the hallway for families to view that he continues to create drawings. Knowing that Azizi does not often visit the art area, Ms. Grace makes the most of these opportunities to document his work with follow-up documentation panels. Several weeks later, Azizi tells Ms. Grace that he has a great idea: he wants to collect his drawings to create a book of stories.

It is evident that Ms. Grace knows the children in her class well. Her documentation always happens when children are engaged in everyday tasks. Knowing both Madison's and Azizi's temperaments and personalities, she is mindful that Madison often plays by herself and likes to pretend to be the adult. She realizes that if she asks Madison what she is doing, she will become self-conscious and may stop what she is doing. Ms. Grace is also aware that if she attempts to talk to Azizi she might distract him. Instead, she uses a camera to document Azizi's truck driver drawing. Both Madison and Azizi have given Ms. Grace a wealth of useful information that helps her make decisions about their learning.

After Ms. Grace shows Azizi the documentation panel, she initiates another conversation with him, asking the following questions. She then includes Azizi's responses as a follow-up documentation panel.

### Remember

**Ms. Grace:** What shapes did you use when you were making your dad's truck?

Azizi: Oh, that's so easy. Look! I made one, two circles for the wheels and then I made this long rectangle shape for the truck. But you know what? There are more circle wheels on the other side of the truck, but I didn't draw that side, so I didn't make those circles.

### Understand

**Ms. Grace:** When we looked at the drawing, you told me it has wheels and a horn. What else can you tell me about your drawing?

Azizi: I know it is a really big truck, and it has rain wipers because it was raining when we were in the truck. Oh yeah, and you can't see me because I am sitting in my car seat and I am too small.

### Apply

**Ms. Grace:** I would really like to hear more about your drawing. Why does your dad put tools on the truck?

Azizi: Because he is a worker man, and he fixes things with his tools. He has to clip and fix the wires so that we can use the computers and the lights and the refrigerator. I think my mom actually put my lunch in the refrigerator though, not my dad.

### Analyze

**Ms. Grace:** I remember that you told me your mom also drives a big truck. How is her truck the same as your dad's truck?

Azizi: It's the same because it has wheels and a horn, but my dad's truck has tools and my mom's truck has no tools.

### The Picture Book Connection

*Daniel Finds a Poem*, by Micha Archer

*Look! Look! Look! at Sculpture*, by Nancy Elizabeth Wallace, with Linda K. Friedlaender

*The Looking Book*, by P.K. Hallinan, illustrated by Patrice Barton

*Lucy's Picture*, by Nicola Moon, illustrated by Alex Ayliffe

*Yoko Writes Her Name*, by Rosemary Wells

### Evaluate

**Ms. Grace:** What might happen if your dad forgot to bring his tools to work?

Azizi: I think he wouldn't forget them because then he couldn't cut the wires and fix them, but one day he forgot to bring my lunch.

### Create

**Ms. Grace:** I wonder how you could build a truck like the one your dad has. What materials could you use?

Azizi: I can just use all the different size boxes, and then I can make circle things for wheels. I can do it tomorrow because tomorrow is Wednesday, but not today, because today isn't Wednesday.

# Expand Children's Thinking and Learning by Asking Questions

### 1 Remember
(identify, name, count, repeat, recall)

- What did you make first in your drawing?
- How many circles did you use to make the wheels?
- What colors did you use to draw the flower?

### 2 Understand
(describe, discuss, explain, summarize)

- How are the front paws of this puppy the same as the back paws? Let's take a closer look.
- What did you see (do) on your walk to school today?
- What should I write down about your drawing?

### 3 Apply
(explain why, dramatize, identify with/relate to)

- Tell me about a time you helped your dad (grandma, aunt) cook dinner for the family.
- Where else might you see a car like that?
- Pretend you are a landscaper like Sophia's mom and show us something she does while she's working. (As one child pretends to work, ask the other children to guess what she is doing.)

### 4 Analyze
(recognize change, experiment, infer, compare, contrast)

- What might happen if the wheels on a bicycle were a different shape, not circles?
- What do you notice has changed about our class meeting message board today?
- Now that we patched up the hole in the red ball, how does it feel different than it did yesterday?

### 5 Evaluate
(express opinion, judge, defend/criticize)

- What might happen if we charged customers more money for the pizza at our restaurant?
- What would you say to someone who took all of the playdough and didn't want to share with anyone else in the art area?
- What are the most important features of your Green Monster painting? Why?

### 6 Create
(make, construct, design, author)

- How can you build another robot using the materials in the block area?
- How should we create a documentation panel that shows how we have been creating our vegetable garden?
- How can we create a book that documents the changes we have made to our dramatic play area to turn it into a flower shop?

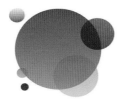

Resources

# Resources for Teachers and Others Who Work with Children

## There's a Question for That!

The preceding chapters offer numerous examples of how to talk with children using questions at all levels in a variety of situations. Here are additional questions and conversation prompts that preschool and kindergarten teachers have used in their classrooms.

### Level 1: Remember

» What color are your shoes?

» How many rectangles did you use in your collage?

» What do we call this place where we're growing our vegetables?

» What shape is this pattern block?

### Level 2: Understand

» What did you see today when we met the builders at the construction site?

» Tell me about the people in your family.

» Describe what you will be making me for dinner in the dramatic play area today.

» Tell me about this part of your block building.

### Level 3: Apply

» Have you ever seen a building like this in real life? Why did you choose this block to use as the door?

» How can you use your body to show snowflakes gently falling down from the sky?

» I wonder how it feels to be a caterpillar growing into a butterfly. Show me with your hands.

» How could you and Marissa change the way you play so you don't get angry at each other when you both want to put the same doll to sleep?

» Our bean plants are growing tall on our windowsill. It looks like it is time to plant them in the garden. What should we do to keep them growing big and healthy outside?

» Now that the weather is sunny and warm, what do you like to do outside with your family?

## Level 4: Analyze

» How is Kailin's pet rabbit the same as our gerbil? How is she different?

» If people wanted to go inside the building you made, which way would they enter? What if a dog or cat wanted to enter?

» We listened to two songs, both called "Going on a Bear Hunt." What did you notice that was the same (different) about them?

» If you chose LEGO bricks instead of wooden blocks to make your building, do you think it would have turned out the same? What might have been different?

» We just finished reading *Cat on the Bus*, by Aram Kim. Yesterday we read *Pete the Cat: I Love My White Shoes*, by Eric Litwin, illustrated by James Dean. How is our story time different when the book has words (*Pete the Cat: I Love My White Shoes*) than when the book doesn't have words (*Cat on the Bus*)?

» How do you think Nikolai feels when you take that car away from him? Can you tell by looking at his face and listening to his voice?

» When the day started, you were really sad and sitting by yourself, and now you're laughing with your friends during music time. What changed from then until now? Do you feel different?

» How can you mix the paint colors (red, yellow, blue, black, white) to get that purple color you used for the sky?

» Tell me how you made that color on your paper.

## Level 5: Evaluate

» These two block buildings you made are pretty similar. Let's play a game! What do you think you would need to do to this one to make it exactly like the other one?

» In the story, do you think the boy did the right thing by sharing his toys with his sister? How do you know?

» If we wanted to get inside this block structure you made, which side do you think would be the easiest to enter through? Why?

» Do you think this feather would be a good material for our game of catch? Why or why not?

» Who would like to talk about something they could do to help our new friend, Trinity, feel like she is part of our class?

Many of the resources in this section are also useful for teacher educators and administrators. In particular, see "Reflection Questions" on page 142 and "Resources for Further Learning" on pages 142–143.

» Which feels better to you, the very smooth playdough or the kind that has the grainy salt in it? Why?

» How do you think the story might have been different if the pigeon in Mo Willems's book had been a goldfish?

» Why do you think you and Keesha are getting along so well today when last week it was harder for you to play together?

## Level 6: Create

» Draw a picture of what you notice happening outside our classroom window. You can use the discovery sheets, clipboards, and different colored markers in the science area.

» Remember, today we are working on creating habitats for lizards. What materials will we use? Where will we get the materials? Let's make some sketches before we start.

» How can you design a way for a car to go inside the structure you just built?

» I wonder how we could change the dramatic play center to become a doctor's office like the one we visited.

» How can we use these recycled materials to create sculptures?

## Anytime, Anywhere Questions

The index-size cards on the next two pages may be photocopied, cut out, and placed around your classroom or carried with you throughout your day on a ring, in your pocket, or in your class emergency bag. Keep them where they are easy to refer to as you move through the daily routine.

## Level 1: Remember
### (identify, name, count, repeat, recall)

What is this called?

How many _____ are there?

What do you remember about _____ ?

What color (shape) is this?

Point to the _____.

## Level 2: Understand
### (describe, discuss, explain, summarize)

What happened first (next, last)?

What can you tell me about the story (block structure, painting, character)?

How would you sort (separate) these pattern blocks (teddy bears, buttons)?

How can you describe the picture (puzzle, block structure)?

Tell me more about that story (friend, family member, picture).

## Level 3: Apply
### (explain why, dramatize, identify with/relate to)

Why did you paint your picture (build your structure, end your story) that way?

Where else in your life (in the classroom, in another book) do you see this?

What would happen if you change the characters in the story (block structure, collage)?

What material(s) could you get from the art (dramatic play, block) area to help complete your creation?

What does your mom (dad, grandma, sister) do at home to make you feel better when you are sad (sick, tired, worried)?

## Level 4: Analyze
(recognize change, experiment, infer, compare, contrast)

How do you think the character (friend, animal) feels? Why?

How is the beginning different from the end?

How does this look different from when you started?

Is this story real or pretend? How do you know?

How can we experiment with LEGO bricks (blocks, art materials) to make your creation stand up on its own?

## Level 5: Evaluate
(express opinion, judge, defend/criticize)

How could he (she) have solved this problem differently?

Do you think the _____ in the story did the right thing? Why?

Which is your favorite animal (story, painting)? Why?

Do you agree with the way that story ended? Why?

How do you feel about your drawing (friend's actions, new baby sister, dad moving away)?

## Level 6: Create
(make, construct, design, author)

How can we solve this problem?

Can you make something that holds pencils (pulls cars, stops animals from escaping)?

How can we create a new song using that tune?

How will you create a story about that?

What ideas do you have for a mural (collage, class book)? What materials do you want to use to create it?

## Reflection Questions

After reading a chapter or two—or the entire book—use these questions to reflect on what you've learned.

### Reflect on Using High-Level Questioning Techniques

1. What kinds of high-level questions do you already ask children on an ongoing basis?

2. What one question, idea, or technique that you have learned would you like to try right away?

3. What would you consider trying within the next month?

4. What would you consider trying in the long-range future? What do you need to make that happen?

5. What was an "aha!" moment for you while reading a particular chapter?

6. Which questions at the end of the chapters seem particularly suitable for one or more of the children you work with? Why?

7. Which of the children's books mentioned in the chapters drew your attention most? How would they appeal to the children in your classroom?

### Reflect on the Book in General

1. Which chapters apply most to the children you work with? Why?

2. What themes reappeared in many of the chapters?

3. Some children's books are mentioned in more than one chapter. How might you use these books in multiple ways?

4. After reading the whole book, what topics would you add that were not addressed?

## Resources for Further Learning

There are many print and online resources for supporting higher-level teaching, learning, thinking, and questioning with young children. Here are some of our favorites.

### Books

Copple, C., & S. Bredekamp, eds. 2009. *Developmentally Appropriate Practice in Early Childhood Programs Serving Children From Birth Through Age 8*. 3rd ed. Washington, DC: NAEYC.

Cowhey, M. 2006. *Black Ants and Buddhists: Thinking Critically and Teaching Differently in the Primary Grades*. Chicago: Stenhouse.

Daly, L., & M. Beloglovsky. 2014. *Loose Parts: Inspiring Play in Young Children*. St. Paul, MN: Redleaf Press.

Derman-Sparks, L. & J.O. Edwards 2010. *Anti-Bias Education for Young Children and Ourselves*. Washington, DC: NAEYC.

DeVries, R., & C. Sales. 2011. *Ramps and Pathways: A Constructivist Approach to Physics with Young Children*. Washington, DC: NAEYC.

Dombro, A.L., J.R. Jablon, & C. Stetson. 2011. *Powerful Interactions: How to Connect with Children to Extend Their Learning*. Washington, DC: NAEYC.

Epstein, A.S. 2014. *The Intentional Teacher: Choosing the Best Strategies for Young Children's Learning*. Rev. ed. Washington, DC: NAEYC.

Genishi, C. & A.H. Dyson. 2009. *Children, Language, and Literacy: Diverse Learners in Diverse Times*. New York: Teachers College Press.

Hansel, R.R. 2016. *Creative Block Play: A Comprehensive Guide to Learning through Building*. St. Paul, MN: Redleaf Press.

Helm, J.H. 2015. *Becoming Young Thinkers: Deep Project Work in the Classroom*. New York: Teachers College Press.

Helm, J.H., S. Beneke, & K. Steinheimer. 2007. *Windows on Learning: Documenting Young Children's Work*. 2nd ed. New York: Teachers College Press.

Heroman, C. 2017. *Making and Tinkering With STEM: Solving Design Challenges With Young Children*. Washington, DC: NAEYC.

Honig, A.S. 2015. *Experiencing Nature With Young Children: Awakening Delight, Curiosity, and a Sense of Stewardship*. Washington, DC: NAEYC.

Isbell, R., & S.A. Yoshizawa. 2016. *Nurturing Creativity: An Essential Mindset for Young Children's Learning*. Washington, DC: NAEYC.

Neuman, S.B., & T.S. Wright. 2013. *All About Words: Increasing Vocabulary in the Common Core Classroom, Pre-K–2*. New York: Teachers College Press.

Pelo, A., ed. 2008. *Rethinking Early Childhood Education*. Milwaukee, WI: Rethinking Schools.

Ramsey, P.G. 2015. *Teaching and Learning in a Diverse World: Multicultural Education for Young Children*. 4th ed. New York: Teachers College Press.

Souto-Manning, M., & J. Martell. 2016. *Reading, Writing, and Talk: Inclusive Teaching Strategies for Diverse Learners, K–2*. New York: Teachers College Press.

Souto-Manning, M. 2013. *Multicultural Teaching in the Early Childhood Classroom: Approaches, Strategies, and Tools, Preschool–2nd Grade*. New York: Teachers College Press.

Topal, C.W., & L. Gandini. 1999. *Beautiful Stuff! Learning with Found Materials*. Worchester, MA: Davis Publications.

Vance, E. 2014. *Class Meetings: Young Children Solving Problems Together*. Rev. ed. Washington, DC: NAEYC.

## Websites

**Center on the Developing Child, Harvard University:**
http://www.developingchild.harvard.edu

**Early Childhood Education Assembly (ECEA):**
http://www.earlychildhoodeducationassembly.com

**National Association for the Education of Young Children (NAEYC):** NAEYC.org

**NAEYC for Families:** families.NAEYC.org

**National Council of Teachers of English (NCTE):** http://www.ncte.org

**National Geographic Kids:** http://kids.nationalgeographic.com

**Rethinking Schools:** http://www.rethinkingschools.org

**Teaching for Change:** http://www.teachingforchange.org

**Teaching Tolerance:** http://www.tolerance.org

# Resources for Families

Encourage families to use high-level questions with their children at home. Here are three handouts you can photocopy and send home with families.

# Questions to Ask About Your Child's Day

Dear Families,

When you ask your child about his day at school, does he often respond with "Good" or "Okay"? Here are some open-ended questions to help start a conversation about what your child did at school. None of these questions has a yes or no answer. Open-ended questions encourage your child to really think about his day. You know your child best, so if there are words your child might not yet understand, change the questions or make up new ones. Try taping these questions to your refrigerator as a reminder to ask them!

1. What was the best thing about your day at school?

2. What was the hardest thing about your day at school?

3. What was the funniest thing about your day at school?

4. What was the kindest thing someone did today at school?

5. Did something happen at school today that made you feel proud? Tell me about it.

6. What book did your teacher read today? Tell me about the story.

# Questions to Ask During Mealtimes

Dear Families,

Mealtimes are great opportunities to talk with your child about the food she's eating, learn new words together, and share ideas. Here are some open-ended questions to help you start a conversation during mealtimes. None of these questions has a yes or no answer. Open-ended questions encourage your child to really think about the meal and other things that are important to her. You know your child best, so if there are words your child might not yet understand, change the questions or make up new ones. Try taping these questions to your refrigerator as a reminder to ask them!

1. If you were our family chef, what would you make for breakfast (lunch, dinner)? Why?

2. What foods did you see at school today that were new or different? Tell me about them.

3. What are some words you would use to describe the chicken (rice, vegetables) we're eating? Let's think of words that describe how it smells, tastes, and sounds when we chew.

4. What can you find on the table that . . .

   . . . is red (blue, yellow)?

   . . . has more than 10 pieces?

   . . . is bigger than your hand?

   . . . is smaller than a penny?

   . . . is shaped like a door (penny, window) or is a rectangle (circle, triangle)?

## Enjoyable books about food

*Bread, Bread, Bread,* by Ann Morris, photographs by Ken Heyman

*Go, Go, Grapes! A Fruit Chant,* by April Pulley Sayre

*Green Eggs and Ham,* by Dr. Seuss

*Rah, Rah, Radishes! A Vegetable Chant,* by April Pulley Sayre

*Spoon,* by Amy Krouse Rosenthal, illustrated by Scott Magoon

*Yummy! Good Food Makes Me Strong!* by Shelley Rotner and Sheila M. Kelly

# Questions to Ask About Bedtime Stories

Dear Families,

Reading bedtime stories is a great opportunity to share a good book with your child, spend time together, talk with him, and snuggle with him. As you read, enjoy the story and pictures together, and try not to ask questions while you read the book. Of course, it is okay if your child interrupts to comment or ask questions. Ask questions before you read, to get your child ready for the story, and after you read, to discuss the story and your child's thoughts about it.

Here are a few tips:

» Any good children's book can be a good bedtime story! Read books that both you and your child enjoy. The more you love the book, the more enthusiasm you will have when you read it.

» If your child doesn't seem interested in a book, put it away. It may be too long, too wordy, or just not a good fit for your child. You can try the book again another time.

» If your child asks for the same book over and over again, that's fine. Hearing a book read many times helps build listening and reading skills. Knowing a story well may also give your child a sense of confidence. Just ask some new questions to keep it interesting.

» Books can be expensive, but you don't have to buy them. Go to the library with your child—it is one of the best treasures your community has to offer!

Questions to ask **before** you read the story:

1. What do you think the story will be about? (Look at the front and back covers.)

2. What do you think the characters in the story will be like?

3. Where do you think the story will take place?

4. Do you think this will be a story that really happened (nonfiction) or a pretend story (fiction)?

5. What does the illustration on the front cover make you think of? How does it make you feel?

Questions to ask **after** you read the story:

1. What did you think about the story?

2. What was your favorite part?

3. Can you think of a different ending? What would it be?

4. If you had written (illustrated) the story, what would you have done differently?

5. If you were going to write a sequel to the book, what would happen next?

## Some favorite bedtime books

*"More More More," Said the Baby*, by Vera B. Williams

*Time for Bed*, by Mem Fox, illustrated by Jane Dyer

*Goodnight Moon*, by Margaret Wise Brown, illustrated by Clement Hurd

*Ten, Nine, Eight*, by Molly Bang

*Llama, Llama Red Pajama*, by Anna Dewdney

*Where the Wild Things Are*, by Maurice Sendak

*Go Away, Big Green Monster!* by Ed Emberly

# References

Anderson, L.W., & D.R. Krathwohl, eds. 2000. *A Taxonomy for Learning, Teaching, and Assessing: A Revision of Bloom's Taxonomy of Educational Objectives.* New York: Pearson.

Berk, L.E. 2003. *Child Development.* 6th ed. Boston: Pearson.

Bloom, B.S, ed. 1956. *Cognitive Domain.* Handbook 1 of *Taxonomy of Educational Objectives: The Classification of Educational Goals.* White Plains, NY: Longman.

Carter, M. 2007. "Making Your Environment 'The Third Teacher.'" *Exchange* 176 (July/August): 22–26.

Copple, C., & S. Bredekamp. 2006. *Basics of Developmentally Appropriate Practice: An Introduction for Teachers of Children 3 to 6.* Washington, DC: NAEYC.

Derman-Sparks, L., & J.O. Edwards. 2010. *Anti-Bias Education for Young Children and Ourselves.* Washington, DC: NAEYC.

Eisner, E.W. 2004. *The Arts and the Creation of Mind.* New Haven, CT: Yale University Press.

Fusco, E. 2012. *Effective Questioning Strategies in the Classroom: A Step-by-Step Approach to Engaged Thinking and Learning, K–8.* New York: Teachers College Press.

Galinsky, E., & N. Gardner. 2017. "Good Guidance: The 7 Essential Life Skills—Skill 5: Critical Thinking." *Teaching Young Children* 10 (2): 5–7.

Griss, S. "The Power of Movement in Teaching and Learning." *Education Week,* March 20, 2013. http://www.edweek.org/tm/articles/2013/03/19/fp_griss.html.

Hansel, R.R. 2015. "Bringing Blocks Back to the Kindergarten Classroom." *Young Children* 70 (1): 44–51.

Hansel, R.R. 2017. *Creative Block Play: A Comprehensive Guide to Learning through Building.* St. Paul, MN: Redleaf Press.

Harms, T., R.M. Clifford, & D. Cryer. 2014. *Early Childhood Environment Rating Scale.* 3rd ed. (ECERS-3). New York: Teachers College Press.

Jalongo, M.R. 2008. *Learning to Listen, Listening to Learn: Building Essential Skills in Young Children.* Washington, DC: NAEYC.

Malaguzzi, L. 1993. "History, Ideas, and Basic Philosophy." In *The Hundred Languages of Children: The Reggio Emilia Approach to Early Childhood Education,* eds. C. Edwards, L. Gandini, & G. Forman, 41–90. Norwood, NJ: Ablex Publishing.

McLennan, D.P. 2017. "Math Learning—and a Touch of Science—in the Outdoor World." *Teaching Young Children* 10 (4): 19–22. http://www.naeyc.org/tyc/article/math-science-outdoor.

Mufson, L., & J. Strasser. 2016. "'Not All Done, Just Done for Today!' Using Multiday Creative Explorations and Bloom's Taxonomy to Extend Preschoolers' Thinking." *Teaching Young Children* 9 (3): 19–21.

Nemeth, K.N. 2012. *Basics of Supporting Dual Language Learners: An Introduction for Educators of Children from Birth through Age 8.* Washington, DC: NAEYC.

Ramsey, P.G. 2015. *Teaching and Learning in a Diverse World: Multicultural Education for Young Children.* 4th ed. New York: Teachers College Press.

Souto-Manning, M. 2013. *Multicultural Teaching in the Early Childhood Classroom: Approaches, Strategies and Tools, Preschool–2nd Grade.* New York: Teachers College Press.

Torbert, M., & L.B. Schneider. 1993. *Follow Me Too: A Handbook of Movement Activities for Three- To Five-Year-Olds.* Boston, MA: Addison-Wesley.

Tunks, K.W. 2009. "Block Play: Practical Suggestions for Common Dilemmas." *Dimensions of Early Childhood* 37 (1): 3–8.

Vance, E. 2014. *Class Meetings: Young Children Solving Problems Together.* Rev. ed. Washington, DC: NAEYC.

# Acknowledgments

We so appreciate all of our mentors, colleagues, and, of course, the children who have inspired us to share our ideas about scaffolding learning through high-level questioning. As we've often said, "Our heads are filled with children!" Derry Koralek, thank you for encouraging us to write the original five articles about high-level questions when we first proposed writing just one. Kathy Charner and Holly Bohart, thank you for your wonderful editing. Your thoughtful comments helped us refine our words and connect the threads of our thinking that weave their way through the book. To our colleagues who wrote the invited chapters, we are proud to have worked with you and are grateful for your added perspectives. Holly Seplocha, there is no better friend, colleague, and visionary!

Kathi Rodger-Sachs, your perceptive reading of an early draft of the book was so helpful. Emily Vance, many years of using your *Class Meetings* book brought so much insight into how to listen to children. Ann Morris and Polly Greenberg, your writing voices were such inspirations to Janis. Leslie Williams, Celia Genishi, and Anne Mitchell, you were professors who got to the heart of high-level thinking. Jared and Jason, your mom still likes to ask lots of questions!

For Lisa, her family—especially her father's constant urging to "Stay on it!"—has kept her driving forward through every phase of life, both professionally and personally. Heela Sarwary, your motivation and encouragement were also great inspiration to Lisa when she first began to entertain the idea of bringing this concept of Bloom's Taxonomy out of her own classroom and onto the pages of TYC.

To our spouses, Rob and Jason, whose love and encouragement we are so lucky to have. Thanks for understanding our preoccupation with writing. Finally, to our Levi and Jacob—your mom and grandma will always remember your high-level questions, answers, songs, stories, and poems that we shared together from the time you both began to speak!

# About the Authors

**Janis Strasser,** EdD, has worked in the field of early childhood education for more than 40 years. Early in her career she taught preschool, kindergarten, and first grade; was an education coordinator in Head Start; and taught music in a high school for teens at risk of school failure. For the past 19 years, she has been a teacher educator and coordinator of the MEd in Curriculum and Learning Early Childhood concentration at William Paterson University in Wayne, New Jersey. Janis writes extensively, including many articles for *Teaching Young Children* and *Young Children*, and conducts research on diversity, the arts, and early childhood curriculum. She leads workshops and presentations at local, state, and international conferences and has been a consulting editor for *Young Children*, an advisory board member for *Teaching Young Children*, a member/researcher of the New Jersey Early Learning Improvement Consortium, president of the New Jersey Association of Early Childhood Teacher Educators (NJAECTE), and recipient of the NJAECTE and National Association of Early Childhood Teacher Educators awards for Teacher Educator of the Year.

**Lisa Mufson Bresson,** MEd, taught in urban public preschool settings for 13 years. During that time, she also mentored novice teachers and served on the Committee for Staff Development. She is currently a technical assistance supervisor for Grow NJ Kids, New Jersey's statewide Quality Rating Improvement System for early childhood programs. She has been a contributing author for *Teaching Young Children* since 2008 and serves on TYC's advisory board. She also co-authored a book chapter for Redleaf Press and presents at state and local conferences.

Janis and Lisa share a unique, multifaceted professional and personal relationship. Janis is the proud grandmother to Lisa's two sons, Levi and Jacob. They have been writing together for almost a decade, co-authoring book chapters as well as articles for *Teaching Young Children*.

# About the Contributors

**Ranita Cheruvu,** EdD, is an assistant professor of early childhood education at William Paterson University and a former classroom teacher. Her teaching and scholarly interests are focused on multicultural education, as well as anti-bias and anti-racist teaching and learning experiences. As a teacher educator, she works with preservice and in-service teachers to develop multiculturally responsive and sustaining teaching practices and social justice teaching practices.

**Mary DeBlasio,** MEd, is an early childhood professional with more than 30 years of experience, including positions as a paraprofessional, teacher, director, researcher, trainer, and teacher coach. She is currently a pre-K teacher coach in the Passaic City School District in New Jersey. Mary is also an adjunct professor at William Paterson University's Graduate College of Education.

**Cindy Gennarelli,** MEd, is director of Early Childhood Education Innovation at William Paterson University (WP), teaches undergraduate and graduate courses, and is a supervisor for clinical experiences. She formerly directed the NAEYC-accredited WP Child Development Center. Cindy has written articles for early childhood journals, including *Young Children, Teaching Young Children,* and *Social Studies and the Young Learner.*

**Rosanne Regan Hansel,** MS, is an education program development specialist for the NJ Department of Education, Office of Primary Education. She was formerly an early childhood specialist at Rutgers University and an administrator and teacher in a variety of early childhood and elementary settings. She authored *Creative Block Play: A Comprehensive Guide to Learning through Building,* has written performing arts and learning standards for preschool, co-authored New Jersey's kindergarten guidelines, and facilitates professional development workshops.

**Megan King** is a preschool teacher and has been working in early childhood education for 10 years. She is a New Jersey Governor's Educator of the Year Award recipient and serves on the New Jersey Department of Education's Advisory Council for Teaching and Learning. In her spare time, she enjoys cooking creatively, reading avidly, and spending time with family and friends.

**Sue Mankiw,** EdD, is an associate professor and director of the early childhood undergraduate program at William Paterson University. Her research focuses on teacher education and using read-alouds to support the exploration of equity and diversity issues. She recently had the pleasure of working with preschool teachers and children in an urban professional development school to construct a child-centered STEAM curriculum focused on the school's garden.

**Kristie Redner,** MEd, has been teaching preschool for the past 16 years. She enjoys doing yoga and reading in her spare time.

**Triada Samaras,** MFA/MA, is an adjunct professor of art education at William Paterson University, adjunct professor of art at Kean University, and a master teaching artist with Young Audiences New Jersey and Eastern Pennsylvania. She is a practicing artist whose work has been featured in numerous venues and publications throughout the metropolitan New York City area.

**Holly Seplocha,** EdD, is a professor of early childhood education at William Paterson University, where she teaches graduate courses on literacy, the environment, and research. Beginning her career as a preschool teacher, she has more than 35 years of experience as a teacher, administrator, professor, teacher educator, consultant, director, researcher, and advocate. She is the lead author of *The Essential Literacy Workshop Book* and has authored numerous articles on leadership, diversity, parent involvement, literacy, and technology. She is also a consulting editor for *Young Children*.

**Kathleen Whalen,** MEd, is a preschool teacher in Paterson, New Jersey. She has spent eight years teaching in both preschool and kindergarten classrooms and previously worked for the New Jersey Department of Education. Kathleen's passions include designing and delivering professional development opportunities for early childhood educators.